THE POLITICS OF
GULLIVER'S TRAVELS

THE POLITICS OF
GULLIVER'S TRAVELS

F. P. LOCK

CLARENDON PRESS · OXFORD

1980

Oxford University Press, Walton Street, Oxford OX2 6DP

OXFORD LONDON GLASGOW
NEW YORK TORONTO MELBOURNE WELLINGTON
KUALA LUMPUR SINGAPORE JAKARTA HONG KONG TOKYO
DELHI BOMBAY CALCUTTA MADRAS KARACHI
NAIROBI DAR ES SALAAM CAPE TOWN

Published in the United States by
Oxford University Press, New York

British Library Cataloguing in Publication Data
Lock, F P
   The politics of 'Gulliver's travels'.
   1. Swift, Jonathan. Gulliver's travels
   2. Swift, Jonathan — Political and social
views
   I. Title
   823'.5   PR3724.G8   79-41046
   ISBN 0-19-812656-5

Set by Hope Services, Abingdon
and Printed in Great Britain by
Billing & Sons Ltd., London, Guildford and Worcester

Acknowledgements

Most of this book was written during my tenure in 1978 of an Andrew W. Mellon Fellowship at the William Andrews Clark Memorial Library, University of California at Los Angeles. I am grateful to the Clark Library Committee for the award of this fellowship, which enabled me to complete my work on *Gulliver*'s politics in a congenial and scholarly environment; and to the then Librarian, Mr William E. Conway, and his staff for making my stay at the Clark as pleasant as it was profitable.

It was my good fortune to be at the Clark while Stephen Baxter was Clark Professor and Vin Carretta a Fellow. With them I discussed many of my ideas about Swift and politics, and they took time off from their own work to read my drafts. It is a pleasure to thank them for their help. I am also grateful to Michael Hunter, whose comments on my earliest draft were of material assistance; and to the readers for the Oxford University Press, to whose suggestions I owe a number of specific improvements.

Contents

A Note on References

The following abbreviated citations are used for the standard editions of Swift's works:

Corr. *Correspondence.* Ed. Harold Williams. 5 vols. Oxford, 1963–5.

J.S. *Journal to Stella.* Ed. Harold Williams. 2 vols. Oxford, 1948.

Poems *Poems.* Ed. Harold Williams. 2nd ed. 3 vols. Oxford, 1958.

P.W. *Prose Writings.* Ed. Herbert Davis. 14 vols. Oxford, 1939–68.

References are by volume and page number in the text (*P.W.* iii. 136). An exception is made for the text (but not the editorial matter) of *Gulliver's Travels* to facilitate the use of other editions; reference is by part, chapter, and page of the Davis edition (II. vi. 132).

Classical authors are quoted from the Loeb editions; references are given to the traditional divisions into books and chapters. An exception is Plato, who is quoted from *Collected Dialogues*, ed. Edith Hamilton and Huntington Cairns (Princeton, 1961); references are given according to the conventional system based on the Stephanus edition.

References to the 'sale catalogue' of Swift's books are to the facsimile in Harold Williams, *Dean Swift's Library* (Cambridge, 1932); reference is by lot number.

Introduction

Swift's involvement in political life was marked by some notable short-term victories, but marred by a depressing series of longer-term defeats. What was particularly galling for him was that while the successes were won by his own efforts, the failures were often the result of events and circumstances outside his control. Thus his brilliant pamphleteering in 1711–13 on behalf of the Tory government's peace policy was successful in its immediate aims. But the death of Queen Anne and the triumph of the Whigs blasted Swift's hopes that the peace would inaugurate a new era of prosperity and stability under Tory auspices. Similarly his campaign against Wood's halfpence in the *Drapier's Letters* (1724) was successful in forcing the withdrawal of Wood's patent. But the powerful national feelings aroused by the campaign against Wood were dissipated without producing any permanent improvement in the dependent and impoverished condition of Ireland. The detested Whig government in London was able to re-establish its despotic control over Irish affairs.

A marked feature of Swift's political pamphlets, from the *Discourse* of 1701 to the *Drapier's Letters* of 1724 is a concern to relate the immediate issues and occasions to general principles. But it was only with *Gulliver's Travels*, written in 1721–5 and published in 1726, that he wrote an extended treatment of political questions free from the partisan pressures of the moment. It is too often forgotten that *Gulliver's Travels* is different in kind from Swift's other political writings, even from those written about the same time. One of his lifelong aims, after the Whig triumph of 1714, was to set the record straight (as he saw it) on the events of the last four years of Queen Anne's reign and to vindicate the policies with which he had been so closely associated. But he knew that the only way to do so effectively would be by the writing of a history, not a pamphlet or a satire (he had written enough of those). What was needed was detailed historical argument, carefully researched, and seriously presented as a sober narrative of events. This was how he wrote (or rather intended to write) his most ambitious attempt to defend the Tory record, the *History of the Four Last Years of the Queen*. This work was largely composed in 1712–13, tinkered with at various periods thereafter, but never published in Swift's lifetime. It is not a success, for Swift was unable to escape from his partisan point of view. It is also about the dullest thing Swift ever wrote, for he had little aptitude for writing of that kind. Its importance is that it shows, in conjunction with the other pamphlets that he wrote in 1714–15 (and which also remained long unpublished), how he thought the job of defending Oxford's ministry ought to be done. He knew that neither satire not fiction could accomplish this purpose. The arguments would have to be firmly based on facts.

The political purpose of *Gulliver's Travels* was not the re-fighting of the lost battles of Anne's reign. It was not even primarily intended as a critique of the Whig government then in power. Still less was it concerned with the particular problems of contemporary Ireland. Those and similar purposes were best served by the same kind of political pamphlet as he had been writing since 1701. Swift had a much wider aim in *Gulliver's Travels*: to attack not particular Whigs or Whig policies, nor even Whiggism, but the perennial political disease of which Whiggery was only a contemporary manifestation. Nor did he want his proposals for reform to be too closely identified with any party platform; he therefore focused his attention on issues that were as old as politics—the character of an ideal ruler, the evils of factions, and so forth.

Much has been written on the politics of *Gulliver's Travels*, and there is a vast body of commentary on all aspects of the book. But surprisingly enough, this is the first attempt at a comprehensive study of its politics, embracing personalities, issues, and philosophies. Earlier studies have made valuable contributions to our understanding of particular aspects of *Gulliver*'s politics. Unfortunately the tendency in recent years has been for such studies to become rather myopic, refining on previous commentary without raising any of the fundamental questions that need to be asked. My particular aim has been to devote more attention than is usual to the general political background that informs the reading of

Gulliver's Travels, to give fuller treatment of the knowledge of political thought and European history that went into the making of *Gulliver*, not all of which is precisely definable in the final text of the book. Thus I believe that Swift's admiration for Charles XII of Sweden is as relevant to a study of *Gulliver's Travels* as his dislike of George I.

This study will be found to differ from earlier interpretations of the political content of *Gulliver's Travels* in largely rejecting the accumulated weight of personal and particular allusions that has been read into the book by modern criticism. It may be thought that where there has been so much smoke there must have been some fire: actually it is precisely the abundance of the smoke that makes the evidence for the fire dubious. In place of these overparticular interpretations, this study offers a general reading of the people and events of the political world of *Gulliver's Travels* as deriving from Swift's knowledge of classical as well as contemporary instances of political wisdom and folly.

It is, of course, undoubtedly true that there is some particular political satire in *Gulliver's Travels*. But the true significance of this (there is not really very much) has been obscured by another orthodoxy that is here challenged, the alleged censorship of the first edition of *Gulliver's Travels*. A re-examination of the textual problem proves unexpectedly relevant to the book's politics. The evidence for censorship, reinterpreted here in Chapter 3, reveals Swift (plausibly enough) caught up in 1726 in the heady world of English politics to which he had so long been a stranger and making some ill-advised last-minute alterations of plan and content to *Gulliver's Travels*.

My aim throughout has been to free *Gulliver's Travels* from the dead hand of those puzzlingly particular annotations that have made generations of readers wonder why Swift clogs his general satire with so many topical references. Freed from this heavy burden, *Gulliver's Travels* can be relocated in a wider context of politics and political thought.

CHAPTER 1

The Politics of Pessimism

'Gulliver is a happy man', Arbuthnot wrote to Swift soon
after the book's publication, 'that at his age can write such a
merry work' (*Corr.* iii. 179). *Gulliver's Travels* is indeed a
great work of the comic imagination, the product of what
George Sherburn called 'the infinite playfulness of his mind'.[1]
At the same time it is also a deeply pessimistic book. A true
understanding of its politics requires a delicate balancing of
these elements of pessimism and playfulness. To see only the
comedy is often to miss a serious political point. To neglect
the comedy is to place a misleadingly exclusive emphasis on
the bleakness of Swift's thought. This caveat is particularly
necessary at the outset of a study of *Gulliver*'s politics,
because Swift saw far more in contemporary society to con-
demn than to approve. Much of this study is concerned with
his analysis of political folly and knavery, and it is easy to
lose sight of the comedy. It is therefore necessary to emphasize
that just as the politics is only a part of *Gulliver's Travels*, so
the picture of Swift that emerges, that of a disappointed and
disillusioned man, is only part of his whole personality. But
this is a study of the politics of *Gulliver's Travels*, not its
comedy, and the more serious side of Swift will necessarily
predominate.

A fundamental element in Swift's pessimism was his religious conviction that political corruption and disorder were,
in man's fallen state, more natural than their opposites.[2] Unlike Plato, he did not think that the construction of an ideal
state (whether in reality or in the mind) was either practicable
or even desirable. Thus when, in Part IV of *Gulliver's Travels*,
he created an apparently utopian society, he did not feel con-
strained to keep it within the limits of human possibility. The

[1] 'Methods in Books about Swift', *Studies in Philology*, xxxv (1938), 644.
[2] This aspect of Swift's thought is stressed in Donald Greene, 'The Education
of Lemuel Gulliver', *The Varied Pattern*, ed. Peter Hughes and David Williams
(Toronto, 1971), pp. 3-20.

land of the Houyhnhnms is an intellectual and imaginative fiction, not the programme for reform of the *Republic*. But if his Christian beliefs taught him not to expect too much from the imperfect political order of this world, it also provided an antidote to despair. Swift, like Johnson, knew that man was not 'in ignorance sedate' condemned to 'roll darkling down the torrent of his fate'. The pessimism of *Gulliver's Travels*, like Johnson's, is deeply felt, but qualified.

Swift believed that government, although not necessarily any particular government or form of government, was of divine institution. Describing 'The Sentiments of a Church-of-England Man' (1708), Swift wrote that he 'doth not think the Church of *England* so narrowly calculated, that it cannot fall in with any regular Species of Government; nor does he think any one regular Species of Government, more acceptable to God than another' (*P.W.* ii. 14). So that although *Gulliver's Travels* is a Christian book, it is so in much the same way that More's *Utopia* is. A framework of Christian values and beliefs is assumed, but the actual treatment of politics within the two books is secular in focus.[3] The reality and importance of Gulliver's own religion is emphasized on his return from Japan in his care to avoid trampling on the crucifix (III. xi. 216–17). But Swift wanted to exclude all religious controversy and polemic from a book that was to be his most considered political statement. Although we must not forget Swift's Christianity, it is not central to a study of his politics. An account of his political pessimism must instead examine the secular roots of his particular species of political thought. His Christianity he shared with virtually all of his contemporaries. The idiosyncrasies of his mind are to be found in its more peculiar characteristics. The chief of these are his Irish background and his 'Cato complex'. His Irish birth and upbringing gave him experience of quite a different kind of society from that of contemporary England. His 'Cato complex' was a temperamental affinity with, and admiration for, a particular type of hero: the man of complete integrity who is defeated in terms of this world but vindicated by his spiritual triumph. The way that his Christianity re-

---

[3] I am unable to take seriously the religious interpretations advanced in Martin Kallich, *The Other End of the Egg* (Bridgeport, 1970).

inforced his congenital pessimism is illustrated by the fact
that Christ himself is a notable example of such a hero. But
Swift was no saint or mystic, and he looked to secular
examples as guides for his own life.[4]

Swift was born and brought up in comparative poverty in
an unstable society rent by fundamental political and religious
differences.[5] In his own case, this general sense of insecurity
was compounded by more personal factors. His father had
died several months before he was born, and a series of unusual circumstances denied him any normal family life. His
parents' marriage had been, by his own later account (*P.W.* v.
192), rather imprudent, and he was brought up in modest
circumstances aggravated by dependence. He apparently
owed his education to an uncle's kindness. In his fragmentary
autobiography he recalls that at the time of his residence at
Trinity College, Dublin, he was 'so discouraged and sunk in his
Spirits, that he too much neglected his Academical Studyes'
(*P.W.* v. 192).

The significance of Swift's Irish background for his political
thought is not so much that it gave him a sense of inferiority
or psychological insecurity in dealing with his English contemporaries, though in some spheres it was to have such
effects. But more importantly for his politics, it gave him
direct and personal experience of revolutionary instability of
a kind that few of his contemporary Englishmen would have
had. His father and uncles had settled in Ireland as recently as
the Restoration, being thus among the newest, most rootless,
of the alien English racial and religious minority. The tenure
of the English ascendancy as a whole might be firm (though
even this must have seemed in doubt in 1688-9), but that of
particular English families was much less so. Ireland under
English rule had never enjoyed stability for long. Sir William
Temple lamented 'the frequent Revolutions of so many Wars
and Rebellions, so great Slaughters and Calamities of Mankind
as have at Several Intervals of time succeeded the first Conquest of this Kingdom in *Henry* the Seconds time, until the

---

[4] On Swift's 'Cato complex' see James William Johnson, *The Formation of
English Neo-Classical Thought* (Princeton, 1967), pp. 100-3.

[5] For Swift's Irish background see Irvin Ehrenpreis, *Swift*, i (London, 1962),
3-88, and Oliver W. Ferguson, *Jonathan Swift and Ireland* (Urbana, 1962).

year 1653'.[6] Temple wrote this in 1673, and within little
more than a decade Ireland would once more be in turmoil.

Probably the most serious manifestation of Irish instability
was the insecurity of land tenure. Cromwell's land settlement
of 1652 (to go no further back) involved a more drastic
change in ownership than anything known in England since
the Norman conquest. This 'settlement' in turn was largely
reversed by the Restoration settlement in 1662–5. There was
another major disturbance during Tyrconnel's rebellion in
1689–91, although this proved only a temporary interruption.
The whole of the reign of William III was a period of large-
scale confiscations, grants, resumptions, and threats of
resumptions. It was not until about 1703 that any sort of
stability had been reached. In such conditions of permanent
insecurity of tenure landlords (much less their tenants) were
hardly encouraged to pay much regard to proper long-term
plans and improvements.

Swift attached great importance to land as the proper
foundation for political power and as the basis for political
stability.[7] In one of the *Drapier's Letters*, written in 1724
though not published until 1735, he ironically congratulated
Lord Midleton on investing his money in land in England
rather than Ireland. He too would be 'glad to possess a Free-
hold that could not be taken from me by any Law to which I
did not give my own Consent' (*P.W.* x. 112). In Ireland, land
tenure (and therefore the whole basis of political life) was, in
the last resort, at the mercy of the English parliament.

In such conditions of insecurity as prevailed in Ireland
with regard to land, considered the most stable form of
property, the currency was particularly liable to depreciate.
Swift was disturbed by the constant march of inflation, as
chronicled for example in William Fleetwood's *Chronicon
Preciosum* (1707).[8] His particular concern was with the way

---

[6] 'An Essay upon the Advancement of Trade in Ireland', *Miscellanea* (London,
1680), p. 101.

[7] See below, pp. 41–5, for the influence on Swift of James Harrington and the
importance of land in his political theory.

[8] Swift owned a copy of Fleetwood's book (no. 417 in the sale catalogue).
Swift's attitudes to land and the effects of inflation, particularly as they affected
church temporalities, are discussed in Louis A. Landa, *Swift and the Church of
Ireland* (Oxford, 1954), pp. 97–111, 166–7.

inflation had reduced clerical and charitable incomes. The Irish Church had suffered far more than the English at the time of the Reformation. The transfer of property into lay hands seemed to be continuing, and was raised in a controversy at the time he was writing *Gulliver's Travels*. Swift himself contributed a pamphlet, *Some Arguments against Enlarging the Power of Bishops in Letting of Leases* (1723; *P.W.* ix. 45–60). The positive side of his concern is seen in his own generous benefactions to his parish of Laracor and in the provisions in his will for the founding of a hospital. Of course, inflation had been a problem in England too, if not to the same extent. In Ireland it was compounded by scarcity of coin and by the debasement of the currency, particularly under James II.

The problem of the coinage, as a reflection of the general economic ills of Ireland, was amply treated by Swift in the *Drapier's Letters* (1724). In these pamphlets he had also attacked the larger question of Ireland's economic subjection to England, as embodied in a series of acts passed since the Restoration. The Navigation Acts of 1660–3 prohibited exports to the colonies except from English ports and in English ships, effectively excluding Ireland from any share in the trade. The Cattle Act of 1666 laid prohibitive duties on Irish livestock imported into England. The Woollen Act of 1699 prohibited the export of Irish woollen goods, and permitted the export of raw wool only to England and only under certain conditions. Even so moderate and comparatively enlightened an observer as Sir William Temple had concluded in 1673 that in 'those points wherein the Trade of *Ireland* came to interfere with any main branches of the Trade of *England* . . . the encouragement of such Trade ought to be either declined or moderated, and so give way to the interest of Trade in *England*'.[9] These are not matters that Swift treats directly in *Gulliver's Travels*, but their effect on the growth of his mind should not be discounted. He did not himself succumb to the general air of lethargy and torpor characteristic of Irish life, but he was powerfully impressed by it.

One characteristic of Irish society even more important

[9] *Miscellanea* (1680), p. 111.

than the factors already mentioned in contributing to the formation of Swift's political pessimism was the existence (as in France, though not in England) of a very substantial peasant class leading a life of degradation that bordered on the animal. Sir Charles Firth, indeed, thought that the Yahoos in Part IV of *Gulliver's Travels* were a depiction of the 'savage old Irish' (*Corr.* v. 58) that Swift would have encountered in the remoter parts of the country.[10] Swift may have drawn on his experience of the Irish peasantry for the Yahoos (although if he did, it can only have been one of many sources), but he can hardly have intended them to represent the Irish in the way Firth suggested. Swift had pity or contempt for the Irish peasantry, not Gulliver's loathing and hatred. Nevertheless, contact with the wild native Irish was important for Swift in another way, for it showed him at first hand what human life at a virtually pre-civilized level was like. Although he nowhere describes his experience of the Irish peasantry at length, we know of the often degrading level of their life from many accounts ranging from Edmund Spenser's in the sixteenth century to the Edgeworths' in the nineteenth. Spenser's *View of the Present State of Ireland* (written in 1596, although not published until 1633) is a classic exposition of an English attitude that regarded the native Irish as subhuman savages to be tamed like brutes.[11] It had certainly not disappeared by Swift's time.

This experience of the level to which human existence might sink gave Swift a real appreciation of what Hobbes in *Leviathan* had described as the 'state of nature' in which human life was 'nasty, brutish, and short'.[12] Hobbes claimed

---

[10] 'The Political Significance of *Gulliver's Travels*' (1919), *Essays Historical and Literary* (Oxford, 1938), pp. 228–31. The suggestion has been revived by Donald T. Torchiana, 'Jonathan Swift, the Irish, and the Yahoos', *Philological Quarterly*, liv (1975), 195–212.

[11] Much relevant material will be found in the ample commentaries included in *A View of the Present State of Ireland*, ed. W. L. Renwick (Oxford, 1970) and in the Variorum *Works*, vol. x, ed. Edwin Greenlaw and others (Baltimore, 1949).

[12] *Leviathan*, Chapter xiii; *English Works*, ed. Sir William Molesworth, iii (London, 1839), 113. Swift owned and annotated a copy of the London, 1651 edition of *Leviathan* (no. 255 in the sale catalogue). He also owned a Latin translation of *Leviathan* (Amsterdam, 1670; no. 506), *Elementa de Cive* (Amsterdam, 1647; no. 153), and *Opera Philosophica* (2 vols., Amsterdam, 1668; no. 202, annotated).

that although this state may never have existed all over the earth at any one time, there was proof of its reality in the recently discovered way of life of the North American Indians. Hobbes might have come nearer home and cited the Irish. A sixteenth-century account of the natives of Ireland, printed by Camden in his *Britannia*, draws a picture not far removed from Hobbes's 'state of nature' or even from the Yahoos.[13]

Swift usually mentions Hobbes to disagree with him, but his attitude is always one of respect for a worthy antagonist. Thus in the Preface to *A Tale of a Tub* he admits that *Leviathan* 'tosses and plays with all other Schemes of Religion and Government, whereof a great many are hollow, and dry, and empty, and noisy, and wooden, and given to Rotation' (*P.W.* i. 24).[14] Nevertheless, he was firmly opposed to Hobbes's doctrine of absolute sovereignty. In 'The Sentiments of a Church-of-England Man' (1708) he sides with Aristotle against Filmer and Hobbes and arbitrary power, which he regards as 'a greater Evil than *Anarchy* it self; as much as a *Savage* is in a happier State of Life, than a *Slave* at the Oar' (*P.W.* ii. 15). This image is the key to his temperamental opposition to Hobbes, for it was precisely anarchy that Hobbes feared most. Swift is consistently a champion of liberty. Yet behind Swift's overt political convictions, one can sense something of the same fear of the abyss that moved Hobbes: in the treatment of madness in *A Tale of a Tub*, for example, or in the depiction of the Yahoos in *Gulliver's Travels*. For despite his opposition to many of Hobbes's political ideas, Swift concurred with his generally pessimistic treatment of the problems of human nature and society. Hobbes was born in the year of the Armada, and in his Latin verse autobiography he jokingly speaks of his mother as giving birth at once to himself and fear.[15] His political philosophy was strongly influenced by the approach and then the outbreak of the civil wars. An

---

[13] Camden's *Britannia*, English translation, ed. Edmund Gibson (London, 1695), cols. 1042–8.

[14] For an alternative view, that Swift was 'a basically philanthropic man convinced against his will that Hobbes's *Leviathan* is truer to human nature than the Sermon on the Mount', see David P. French, 'Swift and Hobbes: A Neglected Parallel', *Boston University Studies in English*, iii (1957), 243–55.

[15] *Opera Philosophica Latina*, ed. William Molesworth, i (London, 1839), lxxxvi.

Englishman of Swift's generation could remember little more violent than the bloodless Revolution of 1688-9. Swift's own Irish experiences allowed him to share Hobbes's sense of the near approach of life to the abyss of savagery and of the fragility of social institutions, not like Hobbes as a state into which society might relapse but as something close to the ordinary conditions of life in large parts of the country. He did not assent to Hobbes's solutions, but he shared Hobbes's perception of the nature of the problem. The Yahoos in *Gulliver's Travels* are obviously related to (among other things) Hobbes's account of the 'state of nature'. The Houyhnhnms are also, though less obviously, Hobbesian in flavour. The absolutist sanctions which Swift found objectionable in Hobbes's system have been removed from the surface of Houyhnhnm society. But there is something Hobbesian about the grey shades and the intolerance of Houyhnhnm society (this is the authoritarian element that George Orwell noticed and disliked). Hobbes made a profound appeal to Swift in an imaginative rather than in a rational way. Swift detested his politics but concurred in his estimate of and in his image of man. It was not, after all, so very different from Christian notions of man in his sinful and fallen state.[16]

Swift was committed to Christianity by intellectual conviction. His allegiance to the Church of Ireland was, in addition, personal and professional. In the Irish peasantry he saw a kind of life largely unknown to his English contemporaries. The condition of the Church of Ireland (so much worse than its English sister) deepened his sense of insecurity as a churchman and reinforced his pessimistic outlook. His English brethren were more fortunate: their Church (political slogans to the contrary notwithstanding) was never in serious danger. He repeatedly tried and failed to get preferment in England, but it was to the Church of Ireland that his ecclesiastical career was confined. It was not an organization to inspire much pride or hope in its officers. Swift was a severe critic of its shortcomings, and not without reason. Louis A. Landa

---

[16] This aspect of Hobbes's thought is brought out in Richard Ashcraft, 'Leviathan Triumphant: Thomas Hobbes and the Politics of Wild Men', *The Wild Man Within*, ed. Edward Dudley and Maximillian E. Novak (Pittsburgh, 1972), pp. 141-81. See especially pp. 145-6.

speaks of his 'realistic appraisal' of the Church's 'general debility from historical despoliations, of its internal dissensions and vulnerability to external attack, and of the weakness of the Irish economy on which it depended'.[17] When Swift became a clergyman, he joined a profession that was declining in respect, influence, and importance. Additionally, he belonged to a beleaguered outpost of that profession. Even in the small world of the Irish Church, a world peopled by time-servers and mediocrities, his ambitions were repeatedly frustrated while manifestly less able men achieved success and reputation and promotion. This personal experience of disappointment was itself an important factor in his political pessimism. It gave him the conviction that, in the corrupt world of contemporary politics, merit was not rewarded. It disposed him to look for heroes among men whose integrity had similarly denied them the worldly rewards they had a right to expect and receive. Some consideration of his early disappointments and the kind of career he might have hoped for will thus illuminate another facet of his pessimism.

Very early in his career, Swift hoped through the influence of Sir William Temple to obtain one of the prizes of English ecclesiastical life: a prebend at either Canterbury or Westminster. Such a desirable sinecure would indeed have given him a minimum good settlement for life, with the chance of better things to come. By any objective assessment, however, Swift's hopes in this direction were wildly optimistic. At Temple's death in 1699 Swift was 'as far to seek as ever' (*Corr*. iii. 125), nor was he ever to have much luck with his patrons. Swift became, it must be said, somewhat paranoid about his disappointments, disposed to search for personal enemies and conspiracies to explain the repeated failures of his prospects and hopes. His first two disappointments after Temple's death were with his next partron, the Earl of Berkeley, one of the Irish Lords Justices in 1699–1700.

When Swift set out with Berkeley, he tells us, it was 'as his Chaplain and private Secretary . . . But another Person had so far insinuated himself into the Earls favor, by telling him, that the Post of Secretary was not proper for a Clergyman,

---

[17] Landa, *Swift and the Church of Ireland*, p. xvi.

nor would be of any advantage to one who aimed onely at Church-preferments, that his Lordship after a poor Apology gave that Office to the other' (*P.W.* v. 195). A little later he was bitterly disappointed at not getting the position of Dean of Derry. As with the prebend, his hopes were wildly in excess of the realistic.

Swift's conception of the proper sphere of the clergy, and the positions they might expect to hold, was anachronistic. We see it in this early episode and it is evident in his later career. Although there is no reason to doubt the sincerity of his vocation, he resented the extent to which being a clergy-man cut him off in certain ways from the career in politics that he so passionately wanted to pursue. Although bishops had not, since the Middle Ages, commonly held the great offices of state, in the early seventeenth century and again under Charles II the bishops and the Anglican establishment generally had played a more prominent role in politics than they were to do after 1688. The trial of the seven bishops in that year was perhaps the last occasion in which bishops were popular heroes. One major factor in the Anglican decline was that the Church found the Revolution ideologically divisive and even paralysing.

The kind of career that Swift might have enjoyed is illustrated by the exceptional one of John Robinson (1650–1723).[18] Robinson, like Swift, began his clerical career with-out conspicuous patronage. For more than twenty years he had to be content with the position of chaplain to the English diplomatic mission to Sweden, although his usefulness in that capacity was rewarded by William III with both a living and a prebend. But Robinson's chance finally came, and he achieved promotion. After a period of active diplomacy in 1707-9, he was made Bishop of Bristol in 1710, Lord Privy Seal in 1711, plenipotentiary at the peace conference at Utrecht in 1712-13, and Bishop of London in 1714. If Queen Anne had lived, he might have ended his days at Lambeth. Swift was interested in the possibilities of a diplo-matic career. Shortly after his ordination, he showed some interest in the position of chaplain to the English factory at

[18] On Robinson see R. M. Hatton, 'John Robinson and the *Account of Sueden*', *Bulletin of the Institute of Historical Research*, xxviii (1955), 128-59.

Lisbon (*Corr.* i. 16). This might have started him off on the same path as Robinson. Later he took the job with Berkeley, as we have seen, under the impression that it would involve more than chaplaincy work. As late as 1708 he was interested in securing appointment as secretary to the British embassy in Vienna (*Corr.* i. 105, 118–19).

Bishops were likely to hold political office only under Tory governments: it was Oxford who gave Robinson his political appointments. 'How do the Whigs in Ireland relish a Bishop's being Ld Privy Seal?', Swift wrote to Charles Ford in 1711, 'They rejoice at it here, as a Thing that will one day ly against the present Ministry' (*Corr.* i. 258). When, in July 1714, rumours were current that Bolingbroke would form a new and more extreme Tory administration, it is symptomatic of its greater Toryism that two bishops were regarded as possible cabinet members. Robinson was to be a Treasury commissioner, and Atterbury (then Bishop of Rochester) Lord Privy Seal.[19] Had the queen lived and Bolingbroke formed a government, Swift might have hoped not only for an English bishopric but even for government office. Her death blasted Swift's hopes of following in the steps of Robinson and Atterbury.

These were some of the historical and biographical factors that disposed Swift towards a generally pessimistic political philosophy. As an Anglican clergyman he belonged to a group that would exert less political influence than it had. A series of biographical accidents gave him a sense of having been cheated unfairly of rewards that were the due of his efforts and abilities. As a member of the alien English colony in Ireland, he was condemned to perpetual insecurity. Of course, it would be merely reductive to seek only in the facts of his biography for the origins of the political thought that lies behind *Gulliver's Travels*. His pessimism was as much a matter of intellectual conviction as of temperament or environment. It is impossible to be sure whether he came to his convictions through his reading or whether his reading simply reinforced existing ideas and prejudices. We know very little of Swift's mind before he joined Temple's household in 1689. Nor is it

[19] H. T. Dickinson, *Bolingbroke* (London, 1970), pp. 128–9.

necessary, for a study of *Gulliver's Travels*, to unravel the making of his thought. His ideas were fixed long before he began the composition of *Gulliver* in 1721. The purpose of the following pages is not to chart the development of his thought but to illustrate its particular temper and quality by way of a consideration of some of the men and writers whom he most admired and who seem most to have influenced his political ideals and ideas.

Swift's deepest admiration and respect were reserved for the hero of a particular type: the man of unbending principle and integrity who (usually) comes into conflict with his society precisely because his standards are too high for it. He saw himself, and the contemporaries he especially admired, as conforming to such a pattern: Oxford, Ormonde, Bolingbroke, for example. In Glubbdubdrib the Governor evokes for Gulliver the spirit of Marcus Brutus, who reports that 'his Ancestor *Junius, Socrates, Epaminondas, Cato* the Younger, Sir *Thomas More* and himself, were perpetually together: A *Sextumvirate* to which all the Ages of the World cannot add a Seventh' (III. vii. 196). These are all examples of the same syndrome; all men whose victory was won through nominal defeat.[20] An important element in Swift's pessimism was his belief that integrity was almost sure to end in worldly failure. The example of a man's life and death (as with Epaminondas) was sufficient without his writing a word. Nevertheless, there are advantages in selecting for discussion examples of his ideal who were also literary figures. The most important of these are Socrates and Plato, Sir Thomas More, the Earl of Clarendon, and Sir William Temple.

Swift's admiration for Socrates was founded on his personal austerity and frugality, on his playful but constructive irony (like Swift himself, he enjoyed knocking the stuffing out of humbug), and on the nobility of character that was too good for (and consequently misunderstood by) contemporary society. The magnanimity with which Socrates faced his trial and death earned him a place among the greats in 'Of Mean and Great Figures' (*P.W.* v. 83). But it was Socrates' ethical

[20] On the shared characteristics of these men, and their importance as illustrations of Swift's values, see M. M. Kelsall, '*Iterum* Houyhnhnm: Swift's Sextumvirate and the Horses', *Essays in Criticism*, xix (1969), 35–45.

and common-sense approach to the problems of politics and philosophy that earned him his second tribute in *Gulliver's Travels*. Gulliver reports that his Houyhnhnm master 'agreed entirely with the Sentiments of *Socrates*, as *Plato* delivers them; which I mention as the highest Honour I can do that Prince of Philosophers' (IV. viii. 268). The point at issue is the value of 'other Peoples Conjectures, and in Things, where that Knowledge, if it were certain, could be of no Use' (p. 268).[21] Socrates was a man modest enough to know that he knew nothing, yet who knew enough to be able to lead the good life.

The example of Socrates was transmitted by, and therefore inseparable from, the writings of Plato. Swift had in general little value for systematic philosophy (as the opinion just quoted of Gulliver's Houyhnhnm master shows) yet Plato was one of his favourite writers.[22] Nor was it only through his character Socrates that Plato influenced him. In Plato's politics, in particular, he found much that was sympathetic: the sense of the corruption of contemporary political life, the insistence on ethics as the basis of politics, the admiration for the Spartan way of life, the aristocratic and authoritarian bias. It is not easy to isolate the Platonic elements in *Gulliver's Travels*, for many of the ideas involved were modified or reinforced from other sources.[23] But the King of Brobdingnag

[21] This idea seems, actually, to be more Swiftian than Socratic.

[22] Swift's allusions and references to Plato are discussed in Irene Samuel, 'Swift's Reading of Plato', *Studies in Philology*, lxxiii (1976), 440–62. Samuel does not, however, raise the question of Plato's deeper influence on Swift's thought and political attitudes. For a more searching discussion, although concentrating on ethical rather than political ideas, see Hoyt Trowbridge, 'Swift and Socrates', pp. 81-123 in his *From Dryden to Jane Austen* (Albuquerque, 1977). Swift owned two copies of Plato: the great three-volume Stephanus Greek-Latin edition (Paris, 1578; no. 78 in the sale catalogue, annotated) and an edition of Ficino's Latin translation (Basel, 1546; no. 588). Swift's particular value for the Stephanus is shown by its inclusion in a bequest in his will (*P.W*. xiii. 155).

[23] John F. Reichert, 'Plato, Swift, and the Houyhnhnms', *Philological Quarterly*, xlvii (1968), 179-92, perhaps overstates the indebtedness. William H. Halewood, 'Plutarch in Houyhnhnmland: A Neglected Source for Gulliver's Fourth Voyage', *Philological Quarterly*, xliv (1965), 185-94, notes the similarities between Houyhnhnm society and the Spartan institutions described in Plutarch's *Life of Lycurgus*. What the evidence really suggests is that Swift (in common with Plato and Plutarch) admired Sparta and its institutions. For the profound influence that Sparta exercised (though with no specific mention of Swift), see Elizabeth Rawson, *The Spartan Tradition in European Thought* (Oxford, 1969).

illustrates the happiness that results from the conjunction of political power and philosophical intelligence that Socrates imagines in Book V of the *Republic* (473d). Houyhnhnm society illustrates the point Plato makes in Book IX of the *Laws* that a man born with a capacity to attain a perfect knowledge of the good 'would need no laws to govern him' (875c).

Something of the imaginative appeal that Plato held for Swift can be seen in his occasional use of Platonic myths. In the *Examiner* no. 31 (8 March 1711) he introduces his own fable of faction with the myth of the origin of love that Plato puts into the mouth of Aristophanes in the *Symposium* (189e–92e). The slight connection between the two suggests the deep and sub-rational appeal of the myth. Less obvious, because Swift does not signal his use of Plato, is the apparent analogy between the myth of the cave in Book VII of the *Republic* (514–18) and Gulliver's strange behaviour on his return to England from Houyhnhnmland.[24] Just before *Gulliver's Travels* was published, the same image of the cave occurred to him as a graphic way of representing how he felt on his return to Ireland after his first visit to England since the death of Queen Anne. In this brief visit of a few months he had renewed old friendships and delivered *Gulliver* to be published. Back in Ireland, he wrote to Pope and Gay: 'Breed a man a dosen year in a Coal pit, he Shall pass his time well enough among his Fellows, but Send him to Light for a few Months then down with him again; and try what a Correspondent he will be—' (*Corr.* iii. 171).[25] Socrates concludes his analogy of the cave with asking whether the other prisoners, 'if it were possible to lay hands on and to kill the man who tried to release them and lead them up, would they not kill him?' (517a). Of the men under discussion here, Socrates himself and Sir Thomas More had actually paid this penalty.

---

[24] R. S. Crane, 'The Houyhnhnms, the Yahoos, and the History of Ideas' (1962), *The Idea of the Humanities and Other Essays* (Chicago, 1967), ii. 263. Crane's idea is refined upon in Gorman Beauchamp, 'Gulliver's Return to the Cave: Plato's *Republic* and Book IV of *Gulliver's Travels*', *Michigan Academician*, vii (1974), 201–9.

[25] The myth of the cave may also be behind the image of the chained man's attempt to dance in Swift's letter to Ford of 4 April 1720 (*Corr.* ii. 342).

Clarendon was exiled, and Sir William Temple chose to retire to cultivate his garden.

After the death of Queen Anne in 1714, Swift himself was forced into a kind of exile and retirement. But about 1720 he began to think about current politics once more. In that year he wrote the first of a series of Irish pamphlets, *A Proposal for the Universal Use of Irish Manufacture* (*P.W.* ix. 15–22). Not long before he had resumed his correspondence with Bolingbroke, and allusions in their letters illustrate how both men, half in jest and half in earnest, framed their political dilemma in Platonic terms. In Book VI of the *Republic* Plato raises the important question of whether a philosopher or a good man ought to participate in the political processes of a corrupt society (496d–7a). Socrates suggests that since 'there is nothing, if I may say so, sound or right in any present politics, and that there is no ally with whose aid the champion of justice could escape destruction' the philosopher 'would be as a man who has fallen among wild beasts, unwilling to share their misdeeds and unable to hold out singly against the savagery of all, and that he would thus, before he could in any way benefit his friends or the state, come to an untimely end without doing any good to himself or others' (496c–d). The same pessimism informs this image as the analogy of the cave. The opposite attitude to Socrates' was represented by the philosopher Aristippus, whom Diogenes Laertius describes as 'capable of adapting himself to place, time and person, and of playing his part appropriately under whatever circumstances. Hence he found more favour than anybody else with Dionysius' (II. 66).[26] On 19 December 1719 Swift wrote jestingly to Bolingbroke of having acquired a mezzotint of Aristippus for his drawing-room (*Corr.* ii. 332). Replying on 28 July 1721, Bolingbroke took up the reference to Aristippus and the implied contrast with Plato. In imagery prophetic of the manners of the court of Lilliput, he noted that Aristippus 'flatter'd, he crack'd jests, and danc'd over a stick, to get some of the Sicilian gold' (*Corr.* ii. 396). Both Swift and Bolingbroke were mentally preparing themselves for a return to politics, and hoping (as the allusions to Aristippus suggest)

---

[26] Swift's copy of Diogenes Laertius (2 vols., Amsterdam, 1692) is no. 224 in the sale catalogue.

that in any future relations with the corrupt Hanoverian court (with George I playing the role of Dionysius) they would be able to preserve the dignity of a Plato without descending to the buffooneries of an Aristippus.

Their dilemma, whether to risk the fate foreseen by Socrates by participating in the corrupt and Whig-infested court life of England, had earlier been Plato's. In Letter VII Plato tells how his natural assumption that he would take part in Athenian politics was first shaken and then reversed by his sense of the corruption of the times, a sense crystallized by the events of the trial and death of Socrates (324c–6b). The remainder of the letter is concerned with an apology and explanation of Plato's subsequent involvement in Sicilian politics. The traumatic event in Swift's political life, as the trial and death of Socrates had been in Plato's, was the accession of George I in 1714 and the impeachment of Oxford and the attainders of Bolingbroke and Ormonde that followed. Here Swift saw his own heroes tried and condemned for actions that ought to have earned them the gratitude of their country. His disgust is recorded in *Gulliver's Travels* when in Glubbdubdrib Gulliver finds that most of those who performed 'some great Services' to 'Princes and States' appeared 'with dejected Looks, and in the meanest Habit; most of them telling me they died in Poverty and Disgrace, and the rest on a Scaffold or a Gibbet' (III. viii. 200). Under the pressure of such events, Swift withdrew himself into the parochial world of his deanery. When in 1715 Pope wrote to him about his progress in writing the planned satires of Scriblerus, he replied: 'Do you imagine I can be easy while their enemies are endeavouring to take off their heads? . . . I must be a little easy in my mind before I can think of Scriblerus' (*Corr.* ii. 176, 177). This was Swift's period of maximum disillusion with contemporary politics. By 1720 his attitude has changed. The outcome was the *Drapier's Letters* (1724) and *Gulliver's Travels* (1726).

The dilemma of Socrates and Plato, of Swift and Bolingbroke, of any man of integrity who lived in corrupt times, was nobly faced by another of Swift's heroes, Sir Thomas More. More was accorded the distinction of being the only non-classical figure admitted to Brutus' select sextumvirate (III. vii. 196) and Swift was later to describe him as 'a person

of the greatest virtue this kingdom ever produced' (*P.W.* xiii.
123). More's personal frugality, generosity, talent for friendship, political rectitude, inflexible incorruptability (he left
office as poor as he entered it), and the heroic firmness of his
end (celebrated in 'Of Mean and Great Figures', *P.W.* v. 84)
comprise a cluster of the virtues that Swift most admired.
They were thrown into bold relief by their exercise in an
exceptionally black period of English history, the despotic
tyranny of one of the chief villains in Swift's historical
demonology, Henry VIII.[27]

The case of Sir Thomas More is particularly relevant to
Gulliver's Travels, for there are illuminating parallels not only
between *Gulliver* and *Utopia* but between the occasions and
genesis of the two works. Swift's conception of the good
society has much in common with More's.[28] In many ways
Gulliver's Travels is closer to *Utopia* than to Plato's *Republic*.
Government for More and Swift is ideally a less specialized
affair than it is for Plato. They believe in no class of specially
trained administrators, while their societies are peaceful and
paternally structured against Plato's communal militaristic
aristocracy in the *Republic*. When we come to consider
specific resemblances between the two works, many of the
ideas involved are too commonplace for one to regard *Utopia*
as a definite source for *Gulliver's Travels*, but the cluster of
similar ideas is evidence of affinity and sympathy of thought.
Thus More, like Swift, treats war as a madness of kings.[29] The

[27] See Swift's vituperative marginalia (*P.W.* v. 247-51) on Herbert's *Life and
Raigne of Henry VIII* (London, 1649); also Landa, *Swift and the Church of
Ireland*, pp. 159-64.

[28] A copy of *Utopia* (Amsterdam, 1631) appears in a list of his books that
Swift drew up in 1715, although (strangely enough) no work by More appears in
the 1745 sale catalogue. The 1715 list is reprinted in T. P. Le Fanu, 'Catalogue of
Dean Swift's Library in 1715, with an Inventory of his Personal Property in
1742', *Proceedings of the Royal Irish Academy*, Series C, xxxvii (1927), 263-74;
'Eutopia' appears on p. 272. In 'A Voyage to Nowhere with Thomas More and
Jonathan Swift', *Sewanee Review*, lxix (1961), 534-65, John Traugott discusses
the relationship between *Utopia* and *Gulliver's Travels*. He has most to say about
Part IV. The presence in *Gulliver's Travels* of both Plato and More is assessed, as
part of a subtle and wide-ranging argument, by Jenny Mezciems, 'The Unity of
Swift's "Voyage to Laputa": Structure and Meaning in Utopian Fiction', *Modern
Language Review*, lxxii (1977), 1-21.

[29] *Utopia*, ed. Edward Surtz and J. H. Hexter (New Haven, 1965; Yale ed. of
Complete Works, vol. 4), pp. 87-9, 97, 205. Subsequent references in the text are
to this edition.

futility of conquest is illustrated in *Utopia* by the story of
the Achorians, a people who won a second realm for their
king but who finally forced him to choose between the two
kingdoms 'because the king, being distracted with the charge
of two kingdoms, could not properly attend to either' (pp.
89–91). There is a lesson here both for the Emperor of Lilliput (I. v. 53) and for such monarchs of more than one
country as George I, King of England and Elector of Hanover.
The Utopians, like the Brobdingnagians, have few laws (p.
195; *Gulliver's Travels*, II. vii. 136). The first business of the
Utopian senate is to 'determine what commodity is in plenty
in each particular place and again where on the island the
crops have been meager. They at once fill up the scarcity of
one place by the surplus of another' (p. 147). Similarly at the
Houyhnhnm assembly 'they inquire into the State and Condition of the several Districts; whether they abound or be
deficient in Hay or Oats, or Cows or *Yahoos*? And where-ever
there is any Want (which is but seldom) it is immediately
supplied by unanimous Consent and Contribution' (IV. viii.
270). Like Machiavelli, who was writing about the same time,
More attacks mercenary troops and standing armies (pp. 65,
149–51, 209). So does the King of Brobdingnag (II. vi. 131).[30]

The second kind of parallel is that both *Utopia* and
Gulliver's Travels were written at a fruitful junction between
disengagement and commitment.[31] In May 1515 More, from
a busy legal practice, was appointed one of a team of envoys
to settle a commercial treaty with the Spanish Netherlands.
In mid-July these negotiations were recessed and More was
free to enjoy some months of unexpected and unwonted
leisure. *Utopia* was conceived and begun at this time. In
October More was recalled to London and offered a post in
the royal service, which he was eventually to accept. It was
not until September 1516 that the completed manuscript of
Utopia was sent to Erasmus for publication at Louvain. In
the interim More had added a large part of what now forms
Book I, the imaginary conversation between More himself,

---

[30] The attack on standing armies is also characteristic of Harrington and later
'country' party ideology; see below, pp. 44–5.

[31] For the composition of *Utopia*, see J. H. Hexter, Introduction, pp. xv–xxiii,
xxvii–xli.

Peter Giles, and the fictional Raphael Hythlodaeus on just
the problem that had exercised Socrates and Plato and was
in 1720–6 to exercise Swift and Bolingbroke: whether the
philosopher should take part in state affairs. In this imaginary
dialogue, More himself puts the case for participation. He
argues that 'you must not abandon the ship in a storm because
you cannot control the winds' (p. 99). Hythlodaeus, on the
other hand, follows Plato in thinking that 'philosophers are
right in abstaining from administration of the commonwealth.
They observe the people rushing out into the streets and being
soaked by constant showers and cannot induce them to go
indoors and escape the rain. They know that, if they go out,
they can do no good but will only get wet with the rest'
(p. 103). The powerful impact of the dialogue derives much
of its force from its context in More's own political dilemma,
whether or not to join the royal service of Henry VIII.

Although *Gulliver's Travels* does not precisely belong to
the genre of 'advice to a ruler' represented in its purest form
by Machiavelli's *Prince*, it is in part a kind of statesman's
handbook in the way that *Utopia* is. Like *Utopia*, it was
written at a propitious juncture in its author's life. Its composition was more extended but spanned a similar period of
suspension between political non-commitment and participation. Its conception belongs to the period of leisure and
reflection that followed the death of Queen Anne in 1714,
years that gave Swift the opportunity to reflect on his
political ideas and philosophy that had been denied him
while caught up in the day-to-day affairs of political life
between 1710 and 1714. But by about 1720 he had begun to
turn his thoughts back to contemporary politics and to the
possibility of his again taking a leading and active part in
them. His 'Letter to Pope', dated 10 January 1721 is a retro-
spective testament of his political belief (*P.W.* ix. 25). Three
months later, he wrote to Charles Ford announcing that he
had begun work on what was to become *Gulliver's Travels*
(*Corr.* ii. 381). Between then and the completion of *Gulliver*
in 1725 Swift became very much involved in the politics of
Ireland, especially through the *Drapier's Letters* (1724). In
1725 Bolingbroke returned to England, and in 1726 Swift
himself revisited England for the first time since the death of

Queen Anne. He had no intention of doing a deal with Walpole. He makes it clear in this letter to the Earl of Peterborough of 28 April 1726 that his recent interview with Walpole was 'without any view to myself' but on behalf of Ireland (*Corr.* iii. 131–5). But whether he might take part with Bolingbroke in some kind of political opposition activity must have been an open question in his mind as he finished, revised, and transcribed *Gulliver's Travels*. It is not easy to specify precisely the ways in which the favourable biographical conjuncture affected *Gulliver*, further than to suggest that (as with *Utopia*) it may have been ultimately responsible for the book's greatness.[32]

In Swift's personal martyrology, Clarendon occupied a place scarcely inferior to that of More. Like More, Clarendon was a man of broad humanistic interests who had enjoyed the friendship of most of the best writers and thinkers of his day. Like More, he had taken part in the world of practical politics, with all its perils for the man of integrity. His career followed a similar pattern to More's. Clarendon suffered exile for his royalist principles and loyalties in 1646–60 and again after 1667. Under Charles II, as under Henry VIII, the man who deserved the highest honours of the state found himself deserted and disgraced by an ungrateful king.

Clarendon's political ideas and historical thought, like his character and career, were congenial to Swift's own. After the publication of his *History of the Rebellion* in 1702–4 Clarendon became something of a patron saint to the Tories.[33] But Swift had also personal and particular reasons for his admiration for Clarendon. Clarendon's historical thought, with its emphasis on moral analysis and the importance of personality, had much in common with Swift's own. Swift would also have drawn a parallel between his own shift of party loyalty in

[32] Swift's re-involvement in English politics resulted in some loss as well as this large gain, as I argue below, pp. 68–70, 79–80.

[33] Swift's annotated copy of Clarendon's *History of the Rebellion* (3 vols., Oxford, 1707; no. 238 in the sale catalogue) is now in Archbishop Marsh's Library, Dublin. The marginalia are disappointing, mainly recording Swift's anti-Scottish prejudices (*P.W.* v. 295–320). When Sir Walter Scott examined the set, however, a note on the first board read 'Finished the 4th time, April 18, 1741' (*P.W.* v. 295). This note has since been lost through rebinding. Swift's particular value for the set is indicated by its inclusion in the same legacy as his Stephanus Plato (n. 17 above).

1708–10 and Clarendon's joining the king's party in 1641.[34]
In Clarendon's view, parliament had deserted him; just as
Swift regarded the Whigs as having left him rather than himself as having left the Whigs. Clarendon was also, especially
after the Restoration, a nostalgic conservative. His desire to
return to the good old days of Charles I's reign (before the
troubles with parliament) led him both to oppose administra-
tive reform and to ignore such new constitutional realities as
the need to 'manage' parliament.[35] Swift, like Clarendon,
believed in the ideal of an independent House of Commons
that would, left to itself and without ministerial interference
or corruption, naturally support the government while it
pursued policies that were clearly in the national interest.
Both men looked back to the more ordered and hierarchical
society that had existed (in their minds at least) before the
civil wars. The powerful appeal to Swift of Clarendon's
History was as a chronicle of the breakup of that good
society.

Clarendon's *History* served Swift in another way, too, for
as an Anglican he was practically committed to a virtual cult
of Charles I and as an Anglican clergyman to preaching
occasional sermons on 30 January (the fast day ordained to
commemorate Charles's martyrdom). One of the very few of
Swift's sermons to survive is one probably delivered on
30 January 1726 (*P.W.* ix. 219–31). Swift was no admirer of

[34] 'To Hyde, to Falkland, and to Colepepper, as framers of these royal mani-
festoes, belongs the praise, that, in advocating a newly adopted cause, they were
still true to their former principles; that in defending the party of the King, they
still contended for the liberties of the people; and while endeavouring to raise the
humbled prerogative, they attempted to restrain it from exceeding those limits
which the voice of the nation had prescribed.' T. H. Lister, *Life and Administration
of Edward, First Earl of Clarendon*, i (London, 1838), 184.

[35] For a brief account of Clarendon that emphasizes his post-Restoration conservatism, see J. R. Jones, *Country and Court: England 1658–1714* (London,
1978), pp. 16–17, 154–62. This was the side of Clarendon that Swift admired, but
it was not the whole man. Hugh Trevor-Roper, for example, speaking of Clarendon's participation in the intellectual circle that gathered round Lord Falkland at
Tew, notes that 'he wrote down his "cursory and occasional considerations", some
of which would be very surprising to those who see him an an archaic, backward-
looking conservative in a context in which, by definition, the Puritans are the
Moderns. For in his philosophy Hyde is essentially a modern, a Baconian. He constantly quotes Bacon . . .' ('Clarendon', *Times Literary Supplement*, 10 January
1975, p. 32).

Charles's absolutist tendencies, and the sermon is remarkably restrained in what it says about Charles.[36] Swift used the occasion to preach a political doctrine not essentially different from his 'Sentiments of a Church-of-England Man' (1708). It was largely through the sympathetic portrait in Clarendon's *History* that Swift was able to view Charles as a great and good man, too good in fact for his times, and to idealize the peaceful part of his reign as the final flowering of the old England he admired and regretted. Thus Clarendon contributed powerfully to the formation of Swift's sense of the decline and degeneracy of modern England.

With the last figure to be considered here, Sir William Temple, we come to Swift's own experience of politics as distinct from his second-hand experience through reading about it. The ten years, from 1689 to 1699, that Swift spent in Temple's orbit were largely spent in England in what must have been exciting and congenial surroundings.[37] After the comparative isolation of student life in Dublin, Swift was able to meet the king and many of the politically active notables of the country. For all this, in more than one way Swift's residence with Temple deepened the pessimistic cast of his political thought. For the retired Temple whom Swift knew was a man profoundly disillusioned with the contemporary world and how it had treated him. He had taken refuge from politics and corruption in reading and gardening. His political views were conservative and paternalistic, out of sympathy with most of what was regarded as 'modern'. If it was not already part of his make-up, Swift would have learned his contempt for the mere success of the world from Temple.

'I never read his writings but I prefer him to all others at present in England, Which I suppose is all but a piece of self-love, and the likeness of humors makes one fond of them as if they were ones own' (*Corr*. i. 10). Thus Temple appeared

---

[36] On the genre and context of this sermon, see E. W. Rosenheim, Jr., 'Swift and the Martyred Monarch', *Philological Quarterly*, liv (1975), 178–94. Rosenheim notes that its tone and content are closer to *Gulliver's Travels* than to traditional Tory 30 January sermons (p. 191). One trait that Swift found to admire in Charles I was his patronage of learning (*P.W.* iv. 9).

[37] The best general account of Swift's relationship to Temple is in Ehrenpreis, *Swift*, i. 91–182, 247–64. The best study of Temple himself is Homer E. Woodbridge, *Sir William Temple* (New York, 1940).

to Swift in 1692, writing to his cousin Thomas. What is
worth noticing is not so much the youthful admiration
(which would have been natural enough) for Temple's writings
but the imputed 'likeness of humors', hardly to be expected
between two men thirty years apart in age and worlds apart
in experience of life. Temple was a retired diplomat with a
European reputation; Swift was a young man fresh from an
undistinguished university career. The admiration was to be
expected; the sympathy of mind is 'significant. Temple was
perhaps the single most important influence on the making
of Swift's pessimism and political thought. It was different
in kind from that of Plato or More, for it was exercised at first
hand as well as through his writings and the model of an
exemplary political career. Swift was a member of Temple's
household from 1689 until Temple's death in 1699, with a
short break in 1690–1 and a longer one in 1694–6. Swift was
twenty-two when he joined Temple, thirty-two when Temple
died: an especially formative decade for someone as unpre-
cocious as Swift. The extent and depth of Temple's influence
on Swift is hard to overstate. During these years Swift acted
as Temple's secretary and amanuensis, copying thousands of
pages of his master's writings and imbibing his ideas not only
from these but also from his conversation. Temple's influence
is also evident in the list that has been preserved of Swift's
reading in the year beginning January 1697. The list is serious
in content, without being formidable by the standards of the
time. History and the classics predominate.[38]

The extensive copying of Temple's works must also have
had its effect on Swift's style.[39] The Swiftian ideal of literary
style is close to Temple's. In his essays and writings generally
Temple is content with the general sketch, unencumbered
with overmuch detail and rarely setting forth a complicated
argument or line of reasoning. His illustrations are mostly
anecdotal rather than factual: he prefers the revealing story
to documented detail. All this is natural enough in the essay

---

[38] The list is printed in Thomas Sheridan, *The Life of the Rev. Dr. Jonathan
Swift* (London, 1784), pp. 24–5.

[39] 'Nobody else had conversed so much with his Manuscripts as I' (*Corr.* i.
156). Swift transcribed the *Memoirs*, Parts II and III, *Miscellanea*, Parts II and III,
the *Introduction to the History of England*, and the three volumes of *Letters*.

form (although the last-named habit also reflects Temple's belief that the 'hidden cause' revealed by an anecdote is more likely to be true than a 'fact'). But the method is also characteristic of Temple's historical and descriptive work, where a more factual approach might have been expected. The method is seen to advantage in his *Observations upon the United Provinces* (1673) where his aim is impressionistic. He is not writing a specialist treatise but a handbook to inform (and influence) the general reader. In his *Introduction to the History of England* (1695) the virtual lack of any kind of factual framework would be more of a handicap if that work too were not also polemical and argumentative rather than truly historical in its aim. Without Temple's influence, *Gulliver's Travels* might have been a much less approachable book than it is. Swift learned from Temple to avoid clogging his imaginative creation with unneeded lumber. Thanks perhaps to Temple's gentleman-amateur disdain for the merely factual, Swift did not tell us more than we need to know about the institutions of his countries of the mind. The contrast with a work like James Harrington's *Oceana* (1656) is striking.

Temple's political and diplomatic career followed the pattern that is now familiar from earlier examples: that of the splendid (practical) failure redeemed (though not in worldly terms) by moral victory. It is possible that Temple first set this pattern for Swift, but more likely that he merely conformed to what was already firmly imprinted on Swift's moral consciousness. For one of Swift's earliest poems, the 'Ode to Dr William Sancroft', celebrates an example of the same type but one worlds removed from Temple in other ways.[40] Swift had to look elsewhere than Temple for his religious ideals, and he found them exemplified in Sancroft, the Archbishop of Canterbury who had refused to break his oath to James II and transfer his loyalty to William and Mary.

Temple's first diplomatic employment was on a mission to the Bishop of Münster in 1665. The bishop was to be sub-

---

[40] 'Swift did not agree with Temple in everything. When he failed to do so, instead of criticizing him, he found an embodiment elsewhere of the harmony which he sought' (Ehrenpreis, *Swift*, i. 126). The 'Ode' was written in 1689–92 but never finished (*Poems*, i. 33–42).

sidized by England to invade the United Provinces. Temple
rapidly completed the necessary negotiations, and began to
supervise payment of the subsidy. The longer-term result,
however, was that the wily bishop made a separate peace
with the Dutch. Temple's diplomatic skills, real enough, were
no match for episcopal duplicity. The story of Temple's
major diplomatic triumph, the negotiation of the Triple
Alliance in 1668, followed much the same pattern.[41] This
mission was at least more to Temple's taste: the foreign
policy he favoured for England was an alliance with the
United Provinces against France. Temple personally had not
approved of the recent war against the Dutch. Temple's
brilliant success in negotiating the Triple Alliance with most
undiplomatic speed showed to advantage most of his best
qualities. Above all, the success of the negotiations depended
on the willingness of the Dutch to trust him. Unfortunately
for Temple, the faithless government of Charles II was soon
looking for an excuse to break off the alliance which he had
put together with so much effort and energy. Throughout his
periods as English ambassador at The Hague, Temple's best
efforts to establish and strengthen friendly relations between
English and Dutch were consistently frustrated by the pro-
French inclinations of Charles II himself. Temple's diplomatic
career demonstrated the truth of what Socrates had predicted
of the fate of the upright man in the world of politics.[42]

The repeated frustration of his best honest efforts, and the
generally corrupt state of contemporary politics, led Temple
to a resolution (taken early in 1680) to retire from public life.
Concluding his *Memoirs*, he wrote 'And so I take Leave of all
those Airy Visions which have so long busied my Head about
Mending the World; and at the same Time, of all those shining
Toys or Follies that employ the Thoughts of Busie Men: And

[41] Woodbridge, *Sir William Temple*, pp. 64–72, 80–93.
[42] Temple's one major intervention in domestic politics was prompted by the
same idealism as his diplomatic efforts and met with the same fate. This was his
scheme for a reformed Privy Council, an attempt to bring king and parliament
back into harmony after the scare of the Popish Plot (Woodbridge, pp. 193–6).
Temple's plan was for a council of thirty, of whom half were to be royal officials
and half independent and substantial members of parliament. The new council
was duly constituted, but neither lasted long nor worked effectively. Temple's
scheme was better calculated for Plato's *Republic* than for Restoration London.

shall turn mine wholly to Mend my self'.[43] Such resolutions are part of the common change of political life. The only thing that is surprising about Temple's is that he stuck to it: and his constancy was put to a severe test by offers of high office as Secretary of State. Oxford, if offered office under George I, would have accepted it. Bolingbroke, under both George I and George II, actively intrigued to get it. When Oxford and Bolingbroke affected to be content in retirement, they were making a virtue of necessity. Temple, alone of the men Swift admired, seems genuinely to have enjoyed cultivating his garden. Swift himself approved the example, but found it hard to imitate.

Temple's career showed Swift that the politics of a man of integrity were not likely to be the politics of success. His own career was to follow the same pattern. But Temple did more than provide Swift with an example. In his essays (and no doubt in his conversation too) he gave Swift a rich quarry of congenial political ideas and principles.[44] His *Introduction to the History of England* and his volumes of letters and memoirs are also full of political notions later adopted or echoed by Swift. Temple had been an eager and sanguine young man. The essays, which largely post-date his retirement, remain filled with a temperate enjoyment of the gifts of God and nature. But the later essays are sharper in their attitudes to human institutions, and here the effects of his political disappointments are apparent. The early 'Essay upon the Original and Nature of Government' is optimistic: government is pictured as the benevolent exercise of a quasi-paternal authority.[45] But by the time he wrote 'Of Popular Discontents' (*c*. 1684–5) this optimism had disappeared, as the passages quoted below will illustrate.[46] It was the later, more

---

[43] *Memoirs*, Part III (London, 1709), p. 173.

[44] Temple's first volume of essays was *Miscellanea* (London, 1680); it was followed by Part II (1690) and Part III (1701, edited by Swift). The dates of publication differ widely from those of composition.

[45] Dated by Temple 1672; published in *Miscellanea* (1680). There is a modern reprint of this essay, with an Introduction by Robert C. Steensma (Los Angeles, 1964; Augustan Reprint Society, no. 109).

[46] The date of probable composition is that suggested by Woodbridge, p. 241; published in *Miscellanea*, Part III (1701).

pessimistic, Temple that Swift knew. This Temple might still enjoy a peach, but politics he knew to be rotten.

Temple's philosophical nostalgia is most evident in the 'Essay upon Ancient and Modern Learning'. Since this provoked the controversy that led eventually to the *Battle of the Books*, its influence on Swift is well enough known. But for Swift's political thought other essays are more important. Especially influential was 'Of Heroic Virtue' in which Temple sought to redefine the idea of heroism, denying it to conquerors like Caesar and Alexander and giving it instead to the great legislators and civilizers like Lycurgus.[47] Swift adopted this idea, and it informs (for example) his treatment of Marlborough in the *Examiner* papers. In *Gulliver's Travels* it lies behind the contrast between the Emperor of Lilliput and the King of Brobdingnag. Temple's writings also affected Swift's approach to history. His theory of the paternal origins of political power avoided the objectionable absolutisms of Filmer on the one side and Hobbes on the other.[48] Other Swiftian ideas that can be traced to Temple's influence are the role of luxury in historical degeneration and the *maxima e minimis* principle.[49] But most important, perhaps, was the essay 'Of Popular Discontents', the most extended statement of Temple's political pessimism. There Temple (and Swift came to agree with him) attributed most political ills to the

[47] This essay is of uncertain date; published in *Miscellanea*, Part II (1690); reprinted in *Five Miscellaneous Essays*, ed. Samuel Holt Monk (Ann Arbor, 1965). Its influence on *Gulliver's Travels* is discussed in Gerald J. Pierre, 'Gulliver's Voyage to China and Moor Park', *Texas Studies in Literature and Language*, xvii (1975), 427-37. Temple was not, of course, the first to brand Alexander and Caesar as tyrants. The reputations of Caesar and Brutus varied inversely. The Renaissance idealization of Brutus (rescuing him from the depths of Dante's *Inferno*) was naturally at the expense of Caesar; see Hans Baron, *The Crisis of the Early Italian Renaissance* (rev. ed., Princeton, 1966), pp. 48-78. In regarding Brutus as the hero and Caesar as the villain, Temple and Swift were thus in the mainstream of Renaissance humanism. In *Gulliver's Travels* Swift makes Caesar magnanimously confess that 'the greatest Actions of his own Life were not equal by many Degrees to the Glory of taking it away' (III. vii. 196). The common idea that Swift's contemporaries were particular admirers of Augustus also needs qualification; for a corrective account of Augustus' reputation, see Howard D. Weinbrot, *Augustus Caesar in 'Augustan' England* (Princeton, 1978). Swift's opinion of Augustus is reflected in *Gulliver's Travels*, IV. xii. 293.

[48] *Miscellanea* (1680), pp. 60-7; *Introduction to the History of England* (London, 1695), p. 9.

[49] *Introduction to the History of England*, pp. 51, 284.

'Restlessness of Mind and Thought' which makes men 'for the most part Passionate, Interested, Unjust, or Unthinking, but generally and naturally, Restless, and Unquiet; Discontented with the Present, and what they have, Raving after the Future, or something they want, and thereby ever disposed and desirous to change'.[50] When Swift edited Part III of the *Miscellanea* for publication in 1701, he put this essay first in the collection. Later in the same year he published his own political call to sanity, the *Discourse of the Contests and Dissensions*. Later still, the mood of 'Of Popular Discontents' was to find expression in Swift's creation of the Yahoos in *Gulliver's Travels*.

Learning from Socrates, More, Clarendon, and Temple that the man of integrity, almost by definition, could not succeed in politics, Swift came almost to regard failure as the guarantee of integrity. Temporal rewards, and even the verdicts of history, were lotteries. Temple had written of 'those Streams of Faction, that with some course of Time and Accidents, overflow the wisest Constitutions of Governments and Laws, and many times treat the best Princes and truest Patriots, like the worst Tyrants and most seditious Disturbers of their Country; and bring such Men to Scaffolds, that deserved Statues; to violent and untimely Deaths, that were worthy of the longest and the happiest Lives'.[51] Swift echoes this pessimistic attitude in Gulliver's disgust with 'modern History' in which 'the World had been misled by prostitute Writers, to ascribe the greatest Exploits in War to Cowards, the wisest Counsel to Fools, Sincerity to Flatterers, *Roman* Virtue to Betrayers of their Country, Piety to Atheists, Chastity to Sodomites, Truth to Informers' (III. viii. 199).[52]

Thus Swift was nourished in an intellectual tradition that stressed the achievements and standards of the past against

---

[50] *Miscellanea*, Part III (1701), pp. 7, 13–14.

[51] *Miscellanea*, Part III, pp. 10–11.

[52] Many of the connections noted between Swift and Temple involve ideas that were commonplaces. Temple should perhaps be regarded as a transmitter. But in his edition of Swift's *Discourse* (Oxford, 1967), Frank H. Ellis notes how much Swift's use of classical sources was influenced by Temple (pp. 161–2). Thus it seems not unreasonable to speak loosely of Temple as a 'source' even for ideas he by no means originated when it appears that Swift derived them from or through Temple.

the corruptions of the present. Operating as it did on a receptive mind and temperament, this tradition (exemplified here by Plato, More, Clarendon, and Temple) gave Swift a pessimistic and nostalgic approach to history and politics. It caused him to identify the admirable with the past and to propose it as a model for imitation to the corrupt and degenerated present. Pessimism disposed Swift to cyclical theories of history which would explain the decline of the present while allowing the faint possibility of hope for the future (again, by way of a return to the past). It made him accept, and even exaggerate, the role of chance and accident in history, and it made him admire certain kinds of failure more than success. It remains to see how this pessimism affected Swift's attitudes to the dominant political and historical questions of his time.

CHAPTER 2

The Lessons of History

Swift and most of his contemporaries believed in the general uniformity of human nature. Forms might vary: manners, customs, and institutions were influenced by such factors as climate and would naturally change over periods of time and vary in different places. But the essentials, the basic passions and desires of mankind, were constant. The same virtues and vices would be found, in different proportions perhaps, in modern France and England as in ancient Greece and Rome.[1]

Swift and his contemporaries had a sense of belonging to a civilization with a tradition of inherited political wisdom that stretched back to fifth-century Athens. This sense of continuity informs Swift's first political pamphlet, *A Discourse of the Contests and Dissensions between the Nobles and the Commons in Athens and Rome*.[2] The *Discourse* was published in 1701, at a time when the major political issue in England was a conflict between the two Houses of Parliament. A Tory-dominated House of Commons had impeached the Whig lords who had been privy to the Second Partition Treaty, an agreement drawn up between William III and Louis XIV to divide the Spanish empire between the rival claimants to the throne of the dying Carlos II. The *Discourse* takes the form of a historical dissertation on certain aspects of ancient history, but its relevance to contemporary events was only very thinly veiled. Swift's readers would have seen at once that its real purpose was a defence of the recently impeached lords. They would have known how to apply what Swift said about Themistocles, Alcibiades, and other characters to the current situation. They would have shared Swift's assumption that

[1] For Swift's views on history, see Irvin Ehrenpreis, *The Personality of Jonathan Swift* (London, 1958), pp. 59–82; James William Johnson, 'Swift's Historical Outlook', *Journal of British Studies*, iv (1965), 52–67; and more generally, Johnson's *The Formation of English Neo-Classical Thought* (Princeton, 1967).

[2] The edition by Frank H. Ellis (Oxford, 1967) provides a very full commentary with much material relevant to the study of Swift's historical and political thought, especially Swift's use of the classical historians.

what had been political wisdom and folly in Athens and Rome remained so in the conditions of modern London.

In choosing thus to make his points through appeals to historical precedent and example rather than by reference to abstract principles Swift was typical of his time. It was a method used by radicals and conservatives alike. Whatever a man's political ideas, he tried to support them with historical arguments. And history being the figureless carpet that it is, no one had much difficulty in doing so. The defence of the English Revolution of 1688–9 that is most widely read today is John Locke's *Two Treatises of Government* (1689). But Locke's *Treatises* were largely ignored in their own day: 'their austerely unhistorical approach made them seem irrelevant to the problems of current politics'.[3] Much more typical was the historical method adopted by James Tyrrell in his *Bibliotheca Politica* (1692–4). Tyrrell's purpose was to set the Revolution on a firm basis of historical justification. It must be vindicated not so much as inherently sensible but as an assertion of rights exercised under the ancient and immemorial constitution. Thus Tyrrell devoted what seems excessive space and energy to such matters as the history of medieval parliaments and the nature of William I's title to the throne.[4] Sir William Temple's *Introduction to the History of England* (1695) was similarly conceived as an indirect defence of William III through a sympathetic historical account of the reign of William I. The interpretation of the eleventh century was too important to be left to the historians: it was a question of immediate relevance to the political issues of the day.

Swift did not regard the problems of his age as new or unique, or as needing innovative solutions. He naturally regarded modern history as a variant on earlier historical patterns. The *Discourse* is anything but exceptional in its appeal to history. Nothing is commoner in his writings or in those of his political opponents. The historical content of

---

[3] J. P. Kenyon, *Revolution Principles* (Cambridge, 1977), pp. 17–18.
[4] Dialogues vi–vii treat 'Whether the Commons of *England*, represented by Knights, Citizens, and Burgesses in Parliament, were one of the Three Estates in Parliament before the 49th of Henry III. or 18th of Edward I' (p. xii); *Bibliotheca Politica* (London, 1718), pp. 265–441. William I's title is discussed in Dialogue x, pp. 516–54.

Gulliver's Travels is no less important for being (for the most part) indirect. Where *Gulliver's Travels* is unique in Swift's writings is in the range of its historical reference. Swift drew largely on the whole of his reading and knowledge of history, ancient and modern. *Gulliver's Travels* is certainly, in part, a satire on the political abuses of contemporary England. But Swift was confident that his masterpiece would be read long after the Whigs and Tories had become ancient history, and he was right. He was therefore careful, so far as he was able, not to limit his satire to his own time or country. When he described the party conflicts in Lilliput between the Trameck-sans and the Slamecksans, he had in mind not only the Whigs and Tories whose follies he knew so well at first hand but also the '*Prasini* and *Veneti*, the *Guelfs* and *Gibelines, Huguenots* and *Papists, Round-heads* and *Cavaliers*' he had earlier compared them with in his attacks on faction in the *Examiner* (*P.W.* iii. 162). / Today we could add the Democrats and Republicans and other examples from modern societies, for despite the fact that we no longer share Swift's belief in the uniformity of human nature, *Gulliver's Travels* remains surprisingly relevant to the politics of the twentieth century. It has even been suggested that it is easier to understand eighteenth-century British politics through those of the contemporary United States than through those of modern Britain.[5] This relevance is not merely a corollary of *Gulliver's Travels* being a great work of imaginative literature and therefore transcending its historical milieu. It was consciously built in by Swift himself. His method in *Gulliver's Travels* was to create types or paradigms, whether of individuals, institutions, or societies. These paradigms are based, of course, on his knowledge of actual examples. But it is misleading to search for originals or prototypes: history illustrates *Gulliver's Travels*, it does not explain it.

Swift was most familiar with English history, and he naturally drew on it for his political ideas and ideals. But these ideas, and *Gulliver's Travels* in particular, need to be understood in a wider frame of reference than the English experience. The historical account that Swift gives of Lilliput, for

[5] Donald Greene, *The Age of Exuberance* (New York, 1970), p. 61.

example, is usually interpreted in terms of English history from the time of the Reformation. It makes much better sense as a general commentary on the European Reformation and wars of religion. Swift did not regard English history as isolated from the history of European civilization. It is noticeable, in fact, in his political writings that Swift more often chooses classical precedents than examples from English history. In the *Examiner* papers, for example, his favourite historical parallels are classical. In no. 16 (23 November 1710) he even manages to combine a jest at the expense of those who 'come upon us with Parallels drawn from the *Greeks* and *Romans*' with drawing his own damning parallel between the rewards Marlborough has received and the accustomed rewards of a Roman triumph (*P.W.* iii. 19–24). In no. 17 (30 November 1710) Swift uses Verres as a peg on which to hang an attack on Wharton; in no. 27 (8 February 1711) he uses Crassus as a stalking-horse for Marlborough. In *Gulliver's Travels* there is never so simple a one-to-one correspondence between the satiric fiction and the object of attack. Instead a satiric figure typically suggests several historical instances, classical and modern, European and English, of the type.

Swift's political ideals can be traced back to Plato. His analysis of practical politics can similarly be traced back to the more pragmatic writers of antiquity and the Renaissance such as Polybius, Tacitus, Machiavelli, and Harrington.[6] Not that there is any clear divide between ideals and practical attitudes: in both we find the same admiration for Spartan-type institutions and constitutional arrangements, authoritarian tendencies, and emphasis on the deleterious role of luxury, a concern for the problems posed by natural decay, a preference for balanced or mixed government, and a supreme role for a wise legislator. Swift's practical politics are, in fact, a logical application of his ideals, not something he kept in a separate compartment.

In Book VI of his *Histories* Polybius gave 'the theory of mixed government its characteristic form'.[7] Swift's *Discourse*

---

[6] See Z. S. Fink, 'Political Theory in *Gulliver's Travels*', *ELH*, xiv (1947), 151–61, and more generally Fink's *The Classical Republicans* (2nd ed., Evanston, 1962).

[7] Fink, *The Classical Republicans*, p. 3.

is a dissertation on the advantages of balanced government, and not surprisingly we find him citing Polybius.[8] The passages of Polybius that Swift cites (VI. 9, 10, 57), praise Sparta for its balanced constitution, equal distribution of property, frugal life-style. Spartan decline is attributed to the inevitability of decay hastened by imperialistic ambitions that its constitution was ill-designed to sustain. Comparing the Spartan government to the Roman, Polybius gives it the preference for stability but awards the Roman the preference as a basis for expansion. A variant on Polybius' analysis is found in Plutarch's parallel lives of Lycurgus and Numa and the comparison drawn between them. Plutarch clearly prefers the Spartan system for its avoidance of luxury, its educational system, its land laws, and an ethos that fostered a corporate spirit rather than an ambitious individualism. The importance for Swift of these treatments of Sparta was that they showed that Plato's ideals might work (imperfectly, of course) in a real state. It was worthwhile to fight corruption and degeneration.

Two particular issues stand out as best illustrating Swift's Polybian analysis of the corruption and degeneration of his own time: the Septennial Act of 1716 and the Peerage Bill of 1719. For in these cases important constitutional issues, as well as personalities and power, were involved. Swift recorded his opinion on the frequency of parliaments in his 'Letter to Pope' (1721): 'I adored the wisdom of that Gothic Institution, which made them Annual . . . while such assemblies are permitted to have a longer duration, there grows up a commerce of corruption between the Ministry and the Deputies, wherein they both find their accounts to the manifest danger of Liberty' (*P.W.* ix. 32). Swift is here expressing an ideal, that the executive should be made incapable of corrupting the legislature. The role Swift envisaged for parliament was quite a limited one (hence it is hardly ever mentioned in *Gulliver's Travels*): it should act as a check on the executive, but should not direct or participate in the executive power. Annual parliaments might seem to guarantee weak central government or even anarchy. This was not Swift's view. He wanted a

---

[8] *P.W.* i. 199, 200, 210, 216, 217. Swift owned and annotated a copy of the Paris, 1609, edition of Polybius (no. 367 in the sale catalogue).

strong central government, but one that would be subject to strict scrutiny to prevent the erosion of the liberties of the subject. 'I believe it may pass for a Maxim in State,' he wrote, 'that *the Administration cannot be placed in too* few *Hands*, nor the *Legislature in too* many' (*P.W.* ii. 18). For these reasons Swift viewed the Septennial Act, which reduced the frequency with which the electors were consulted, as an encroachment by the executive on the legislative power, part of a campaign by the corrupt Whig government to obtain compliant parliaments in perpetuity. This view was shared even by many of the Whigs.

Swift's feelings about the Peerage Bill were more mixed. Writing to Charles Ford on 8 December 1719, he speaks of having 'agreed many years ago with some very great men, who thought a Bill for limiting the Prerogative in making Peers would mend the Constitution' but firmly opposes the present measure. His most important objection is that 'the Lords degenerate by Luxury Idleness etc. and the Crown is always forced to govern by new Men. I think Titles should fall with Estates' (*Corr.* ii. 330, 331). No doubt Swift remembered Oxford's creation of twelve new peers to pass the peace treaty in 1712, an expedient he regarded at the time as at best a regrettable necessity. Certainly he was opposed to the creation of a closed aristocracy on the Venetian model (which would have been the effect of the proposed bill). That could only lead to degenerate torpor. The theme of a degenerate nobility is prominent in *Gulliver's Travels.* Gulliver describes the English peers to the King of Brobdingnag as 'the Ornament and Bulwark of the Kingdom; worthy Followers of their most renowned Ancestors, whose Honour had been the Reward of their Virtue; from which their Posterity were never once known to degenerate' (II. vi. 128). The sceptical king, however, is not taken in (p. 129). Even more damning is the indictment of the European nobility revealed by Gulliver's experiences in Glubbdubdrib, where he discovers 'who first brought the Pox into a noble House, which hath lineally descended in scrophulous Tumours to their Posterity' and the vile arts by which 'great Numbers had procured to themselves high Titles of Honour, and prodigious Estates' (III. viii. 198, 200).

This strong sense of the decline of his own times gave Swift a corresponding interest in the history of the decline and fall of the flourishing states of earlier eras. Sparta, he learned from Polybius and Plutarch, had been ruined by its failure to maintain the institutions of Lycurgus. But the classic case of a cycle of greatness succeeded by decay and degeneration was that of the Roman republic and empire. The great historian of its decline was Tacitus.[9] Swift was not alone in applying Tacitus to contemporary history. Indeed, several of his references to Tacitus are concerned to refute or counter what he saw as improper applications (*P.W.* ii. 29, iv. 27, iv. 82). As these and other references testify, a habit of allusion to Tacitus was commonplace among Swift and his contemporaries. But it was particularly after 1714 that Swift came to identify himself closely with the Roman historian.

Tacitus the man appealed to Swift: his love of literature, his talent for friendship, his aristocratic and elitist values, his patriotism and integrity—all these 'old Roman' virtues. His qualities as a historian were also highly congenial to Swift: his irony, his pessimism, his sense of contemporary decay, his nostalgia for the republic and the age of liberty, the moral basis of his judgements, his treatment of character, his sense of the importance of character especially in rulers. For Swift there was particular poignancy in Tacitus' account, in the *Annals*, of the growth of tyranny while the forms of republican Rome were preserved. For under George I (as Swift saw it) the same process seemed to be going on in England. A corrupt parliament was no longer the guardian of the liberties of the realm but a nest of sycophants and compliers with the times. There were particular parallels between Tiberius'

[9] Swift's library was well stocked with Tacitus. He owned two editions of the Latin text (Antwerp, 1648; Amsterdam, 1649; nos. 393 and 46 in the sale catalogue, both annotated) besides an English translation (no. 289) and an odd volume of a Dublin edition (no. 638). Tacitus was far from originating the idea of a natural cycle through which states pass. The idea is found in Plato (*Republic*, VIII, 546; *Laws*, III, 677), treated somewhat critically by Aristotle (*Politics*, V. x), and fully developed by Polybius (*Histories*, VI, 3–10, 57). Karl Popper notes, in *The Open Society and Its Enemies*, that 'Plato confines himself, when it comes to more concrete historical problems, to that part of the cycle which leads to decay' (5th ed., Princeton, 1966, i. 210). Similarly, Swift analyses Lilliputian degeneration in detail while treating very summarily (II. vii. 138) the Brobdingnagian experience of the other part of the cycle.

gradual and hypocritical assumption of the imperial power (*Annals*, I. vii–xiii) and the accession of George I for whose benefit the most material safeguards incorporated in the Act of Settlement were either repealed or circumvented by a corrupt ministry and its venal parliament.

Neither Tacitus nor Swift was a political theorist. But both men measured modern history against a moral standard that was given historical status by association with the past. Tacitus viewed the Empire against a semi-mythical image of the virtues and glories of republican Rome, an age of integrity, public spirit, and good and disinterested government. This golden age is constantly evoked when Tacitus wants to throw into relief the degeneration, luxury, and tyranny of life under the emperors. Correspondingly, Swift looked back to a golden age of English history before luxury and tyranny had corrupted the social fabric. It is this golden age that Swift evokes in one of the Tacitean passages in *Gulliver's Travels*, the last of the visions that Gulliver sees in Glubbdubdrib:

I descended so low as to desire that some *English* Yeoman of the old Stamp, might be summoned to appear; once so famous for the Simplicity of their Manners, Dyet and Dress; for Justice in their Dealings; for their true Spirit of Liberty; for their Valour and Love of their Country. Neither could I be wholly unmoved after comparing the Living with the Dead, when I considered how all these pure native Virtues were prostituted for a Piece of money by their Grand-children; who in selling their Votes, and managing at Elections have acquired every Vice and Corruption that can possibly be learned in a Court. (III. viii. 201–2.)

In this passage Gulliver is a spokesman for Swift's Tacitean analysis of contemporary change and decay.

Apart from his poetic idealization of the past of republican Rome, Tacitus had another standard to apply to contemporary life. His *Germania* is not a utopia, but its account of the German peoples and their 'barbarous' manners and customs is so suffused with an implied contrast with current Roman manners and morals as to be almost a utopia in disguise. Tacitus was too good a historian to falsify his material: he does not minimize the genuinely barbarous aspects of German society. But he was too convinced a moralist merely to report. When one sets the cruelties of German life against the judicial mockeries in Rome that ended in torture and death, the

Germans do not come off worse. Tacitus thus had two standards against which to measure the contemporary degeneracy of imperial Rome: its republican past, and the more extreme contrast of 'barbarian' Germany. In much the same way, in *Gulliver's Travels* Swift invites us to contrast modern European degeneracy both with an idealized English past (invoked in Part III in the passage identified above as 'Tacitean', and more generally in the account of Brobdingnag) and with the utopian Houyhnhnmland. This is not to suggest that Houyhnhnmland is the same kind of society as Tacitus' Germany (obviously it is not), but Swift uses it in the same way as Tacitus uses Germany, to make a more extreme contrast than could be obtained through even an idealized image of the actual past.

But neither Plato, nor Tacitus, nor Swift was an unqualified pessimist. Plato's experience suggested that the virtuous man could not meddle in politics without coming off badly. Here Tacitus was a little more optimistic. His *Agricola* was intended to show that even under a bad ruler, a good man might do useful service to the state without compromising his integrity. Tacitus himself had served under Domitian. Of course, Agricola was the exception that proved the rule. There were few such examples. The most notable in Swift's own time and estimation was Sir William Temple.

A Renaissance writer who provided still more practical political analysis for Swift to draw on in applying his political ideals to the contemporary situation was Machiavelli.[10] His ideal (like Plato's) was the small independent state of citizen soldiers, and his thought was strongly nationalistic and anti-imperialistic. Where the tone of his thought would have appealed strongly to Swift was in his sense of the almost irredeemable corruption of contemporary Italy, a corruption that Machiavelli thought could only be reformed by drastic measures and a return to political first principles. In his

[10] The lines of thought from Machiavelli to Swift's day are traced in J. G. A. Pocock, 'Machiavelli, Harrington and English Political Ideologies in the 18th Century', *Politics, Language and Time* (London, 1972), pp. 104–47. The essay was first published in 1965. The same tradition of thought is placed in a broader context in Pocock's *The Machiavellian Moment* (Princeton, 1975). Swift owned and annotated a copy of Henry Nevile's translation of Machiavelli's *Works* (London, 1695; no. 374 in the sale catalogue).

Project for the Advancement of Religion (1709) Swift drew on Machiavelli's *Discourses* (III. i) for the idea that 'as there must always of Necessity be some Corruptions; so in a well-instituted State, the executive Power will be always contending against them, by *reducing Things* (as *Machiavel* speaks) *to their first Principles*' (*P.W.* ii. 63). In the *Art of War* (I. ii–vii) as well as in the *Discourses* Machiavelli emphasized the superiority of a citizen militia over mercenary troops, an idea that has an important place in Swift's political thought and finds expression, for example, in Brobdingnag (II. vii. 138). In his *History of Florence* (III) Machiavelli described the struggles between the noble and popular factions in terms of a Polybian ideal balance, the idea Swift uses in his early *Discourse* and again in Brobdingnag (II. vii. 138). Of course, Swift's political thought differed from Machiavelli's in some basic ways. For example, Machiavelli followed Polybius in regarding the Roman constitution as superior to the Spartan because better adapted for conquest and expansion. Swift, on the other hand, rated more highly the search for internal political stability, and had a correspondingly higher opinion of the original institutions of Sparta. Again, Machiavelli admired a man like Cesare Borgia (*The Prince*, vii), whom Swift regarded as a politician of the worst type (*P.W.* viii. 77). But such differences should not obscure the profound affinities between the two men as revealed in their common attitudes to the nexus of corruption, degeneration, and the need for reform that connect their analyses of contemporary society.

Similarly, the fact that Swift would have detested the republicanism of James Harrington should not be allowed to obscure the influence his *Oceana* and the ideas that derived from it exercised on him.[11] *Oceana* (1656) is a political utopia that was actually offered (at a rare moment when a drastic remodelling of the government was a practical proposition) as a blueprint for reform. It was dedicated to Cromwell, a beneficent and idealized representation of whom figures in *Oceana* as Olphaus Megaletor. Harrington's Megaletor is a selfless and philosophical monarch much like the King of Brobdingnag; Cromwell proved disappointingly unlike him.

[11] Swift owned and annotated a copy of the first edition of *Oceana* (London, 1656; no. 381 in the sale catalogue).

Harrington's analysis of political change in terms of changes in property ownership was of particular interest to Swift. Harrington did take account of unusual societies like Venice and Holland that were not based on landed property, but in general his theories assumed that land was the only important kind of property. It was thus particularly calculated to appeal to men like Swift who, after the financial revolution of 1689–1720, looked back nostalgically to a social system in which the power of land had not been challenged by that of money. Harrington formulated the principle that shifts in political power were to be understood not (as Polybius and Machiavelli had done) in terms of an institution's natural tendency to decay but as the result of important changes in the ownership of land. Thus Harrington traced the breakdown of the political system of republican Rome to the growth of large landholdings after the Punic wars.[12] Again unlike Machiavelli, Harrington thought that the process of political instability could be arrested if changes in the distribution of property could be properly limited and controlled. Harrington followed Machiavelli in making his ideal citizens part-time soldiers (he too was strongly opposed to mercenary troops and standing armies) but he made them small landowners as well. In his ideal Oceana large holdings of land could not be accumulated (*Oceana*, p. 164; the influence of Lycurgus and Sparta is evident here); neither, therefore, in Harrington's view, could undue concentrations of political power. The independence of individual citizens would be guaranteed by their possession of enough land to live on (but not a great deal more; pp. 158–9) and of arms to defend themselves and protect their property. Harrington borrowed from Venice (a state he admired for its legendary political stability) the ideas of rotation in office and election by ballot. These measures provided further safeguards against corruption and the exercise of undue political influence.

Harrington approached history in terms of institutions rather than personalities. But his limited knowledge of the details of later medieval English history led him to attribute the decline of feudalism in England to certain specific actions

[12] *Oceana*, in *Political Works*, ed. J. G. A. Pocock (Cambridge, 1977), pp. 188–9. Subsequent references in the text are to this edition.

of the Tudor kings.[13] This interpretation was better calculated
to appeal to Swift's personality-oriented approach to history,
and in particular to his dislike of Henry VIII. Harrington
ascribed the decisive shift of property away from the Crown
and nobles and into the hands of the gentry to Henry VII's
statutes of population, retainers, and alientations; and to
Henry VIII's dissolution of the monasteries (pp. 197–8). These
actions had broken up the large feudal landholdings; the
attempts of the kings to weaken the power of their nobles
resulted, however, in the unforeseen longer-term decline of
royal power. If this process could be continued and perfected
(but then stopped), Harrington thought that England might
approximate to his ideal of a nation of small landowners
officering their own militia and providing by rotation such
central government as was needed. There is much in Harrington's programme that we can recognize as having contributed
to Swift's conception of Brobdingnag.[14]

Harrington's ideas made a greater impact after the Restoration than at the time of their publication, although not in
their original form. About 1675 they were virtually 'stood on
their head' for the purpose of providing the 'country' party
with anti-court ammunition.[15] A group of works associated
with the first Earl of Shaftesbury borrowed such Harringtonian
ideas as his militia and his antidotes to corruption. But they
argued for something that Harrington had certainly not
envisaged, a return to what they regarded as the 'ancient
constitution'.[16] This was a semi-mythical idea of what the
constitution of England had once been like, a historical construct most useful in a period that preferred appeals to history
to appeals to first principles. These ideas are worked out at
greater length than in any of the polemics of 1675 in Henry
Nevile's *Plato Redivivus* (1681).[17] Nevile's work is Platonic

[13] J. G. A. Pocock, *The Ancient Constitution and the Feudal Law* (Cambridge, 1957), pp. 135–9.

[14] Myrddin Jones, 'Swift, Harrington, and Corruption in England', *Philological Quarterly*, liii (1974), 59–70.

[15] Pocock, *Politics, Language and Time*, p. 115.

[16] The attraction of a concept like the 'ancient constitution' for one of Swift's nostalgic temperament is obvious.

[17] Swift owned a copy of Nevile (no. 414 in the sale catalogue). There is a modern edition in *Two English Republican Tracts*, ed. Caroline Robbins (Cambridge, 1969).

mainly in its dialogue form: it is cast as a series of conversations between two Englishmen and a noble Venetian visiting London. The political state of Venice is freely drawn upon, notably in an elaborate system of councils without which the king cannot act. Most of the current royal prerogatives would be exercised by the king only with the approval of one of these councils, whose membership would rotate. In the *Examiner* Swift ridiculed such a 'Whig' system of a 'King, under the Limitations of the Duke of *Venice*' (*P.W.* iii. 122). But many of Nevile's ideas coincided with Swift's, notably his insistence on annual parliaments.

If Harrington's ideas had been 'stood on their head' in the service of the 'country' opposition in the last years of Charles II, they underwent another radical shift after the Revolution. For during William's reign the Tories became the natural 'country' party and the Whigs became somewhat awkward courtiers. Swift liked to think of himself as 'what we formerly called a Whig' (*Corr.* i. 359) and in *Examiner* no. 33 (22 March 1711) he claimed he was 'not sensible of any material Difference there is between those who call themselves the *Old Whigs*, and a great Majority of the present *Tories*' (*P.W.* iii. 111). Some of the old 'country' ideology had been discarded: its anticlericalism, for example, prominent in *Plato Redivivus*. But much of it—support for a militia against a standing army, xenophobia, dislike of placemen—had been curiously grafted on to the remnant of Tory ideology, support for the Crown and Church.[18] It was to this amalgam that Swift owed his political loyalties, a fact which explains the apparent contradictions in his ideas on such questions as the proper strength of the central government. Swift wanted certain kinds of liberty and certain kinds of strictly enforced coercions. It is a convenient shorthand to think of him as a 'Tory', but in many ways it is an oversimplification. If we did not know that Swift wrote *Gulliver's Travels*, on the basis of its political ideology we would probably label it 'opposition Whig' rather than 'Tory'.[19]

[18] For the development of 'country' ideology by about the time of *Gulliver's Travels*, see H. T. Dickinson, *Liberty and Property* (London, 1977), pp. 163-92.

[19] Much of its programme overlaps with the measures advocated by such 'old Whigs' as Trenchard and Gordon in *Cato's Letters* (1720-3). Swift often calls

Swift's loyalty to the Tory government of 1710–14 had been divided between a personal attachment to Oxford and an ideological attraction to the more extreme 'Tory' policies championed by Bolingbroke.[20] This programme was in many ways 'old Whig', although framed as a reaction to the perverted Whiggism of the previous twenty years: an end to the war, a disbanding of the army, lower taxes and a reduction of the national debt, a strengthening of the alliance between the landed interest and the Church. Swift even hoped that time and energy might be found for such pet projects of his as control of the press and an academy to preserve the purity of the English language. The peace was to have inaugurated a new golden age of the new Toryism. In the event it was wrecked by one of those accidents insisted upon so much in Sir William Temple's theory of history: the personal rivalry between Oxford and Bolingbroke and the death of the queen. The accession of George I began a repressive, corrupt, self-seeking regime that added insult to injury by pretending to be 'Whig'.

Swift was not, of course, concerned only with modern England and the Europe of antiquity. During his lifetime England was more closely involved with the affairs and politics of continental Europe than it had been for generations. England played major roles in two large-scale wars, the Nine Years War (1688–97) and the War of the Spanish Succession (1702–13). For much of Swift's lifetime the King of England was also a European figure in his own right. During the reign of William III (1689–1702) England and the United Provinces were linked by a common head of state. After the death of Queen Anne (1714) the King of England was also a German prince of some importance. Since even during the interlude of Anne's reign England was almost continually involved in a continental war, foreign policy was of exceptional importance during the whole period, even to the extent of exercising a determining influence on domestic politics. Direct involvement in Europe was regarded with distaste by

---

himself a 'Whig' (*Corr.* i. 127, 359; ii. 236). For the seriousness with which this label should be taken, see Donald Greene, 'Swift: Some Caveats', *Studies in the Eighteenth Century II*, ed. R. F. Brissenden (Canberra, 1973), pp. 432–6.

[20] Irvin Ehrenpreis, *Swift*, ii (London, 1967), 673–4.

many Englishmen. Swift did not share the average English-man's contempt for Europe. He was interested in European history and politics. But he did believe the English constitu-tion (properly maintained) to be superior to any on the continent, and he thought England should avoid direct participation in European land wars. Swift intended the satire in *Gulliver's Travels* to have a relevance for European, not just English, politics. But as far as constitutional forms were concerned, he thought that England had more to teach than to learn.

Swift's Europe could be divided politically into two main types of state: absolutist (or near-absolutist) and constitu-tional. (The position of the Empire was unique and anomal-ous). One of Swift's most basic political beliefs (and it would have been shared by almost all of his fellow-countrymen) was in the superiority of mixed or balanced government together with a corresponding dislike of absolutism and arbitrary power. In opposition to Hobbes he regarded arbitrary power as 'a greater Evil than *Anarchy* it self; as much as a *Savage* is in a happier State of Life, than a *Slave* at the Oar' (*P.W.* ii. 15). As it happened, contemporary Europe was dominated by arbitrary regimes, and the trend of recent history seemed to be in favour of such forms of government. In Turkey all property was held at the pleasure of the Sultan. Elsewhere (as in Russia, France, and Spain) its tenure was less precarious, but the will of the monarch was still law. In the later seven-teenth century the 'gothic' governments of Denmark and Sweden had been subverted and absolutism established. James II had tried to bring about the same kind of revolution in England. In countries where arbitrary power was the rule, representative institutions were either in decline, in abeyance, or virtually impotent. Such was the case with the French Parlements, the Spanish Cortes, the Estates in Denmark and Sweden.

The constitutional states normally were headed by a monarch with more or less restricted powers. The most important such state was England itself, regarded (especially by Englishmen) as the best-balanced government in Europe. The King of England was in fact the most powerful of the limited monarchs. To the extent that the states in which the monarchical power was more heavily circumscribed were notably less effectively governed than England, there was some justification for this English pride. The United Provinces had what Swift regarded as 'the worst constituted Government in the World to last' (*P.W.* ii. 100). The Dutch Stadtholder (when there was one; there was not when Swift made his judgement) had less power than an English king, while the federal nature of the state decentralized the process of decision-making in a way that could be paralysing.[21] In Poland the king was elected and could not make major policy decisions without the consent of the Diet. After 1652 the precedent was established that decisions of the Diet had to be unanimous: thus a single deputy could not only frustrate particular initiatives but even bring the Diet itself to a halt. The Doge of Venice was little more than a figure-head: he could not act without a majority of the council, but a majority of the council could act without him.

The constitution of the Empire was unique. The Peace of Westphalia in 1648 had resulted in a stalemate between the attempt of the Habsburg emperors to create a centralized and absolute monarchy and the opposing efforts of the Protestant princes of the Empire to turn it into an aristocratic republic. For practical purposes, the Empire almost ceased to function as a state. The Emperor was absolute in his hereditary dominions, but mobilizing the resources of the Empire as a whole involved negotiated agreements with the individual princes. In the struggle between Austria and France, the Emperor was far from being able to count on the support of the nominally subordinate princes of the Empire. These individual princes, in their turn, enjoyed generally absolute sway within their own lands. This trend was particularly noticeable after the Peace of Westphalia. In 1654 and again in 1657 the princes gained substantially in power over their local estates, while the Imperial Diet degenerated into the diplomatic talking-shop described in the letters of Sir George

---

[21] See the account in Sir William Temple's *Observations upon the United Provinces* (1673), ed. Sir George Clark (Oxford, 1972), pp. 52–74. Swift owned a copy of the Amsterdam, 1696, edition of Temple's book (no. 436 in the sale catalogue).

Etherege, English Resident there between 1685 and 1689.[22] The same trend towards absolutism was evident in Scandinavia, where Frederick III of Denmark in 1660–5 and Charles XI of Sweden in 1680–6 had both succeeded in establishing arbitrary power.

It is against this trend that Swift's treatment of kingship in *Gulliver's Travels* must be set. Absolutist government was in the ascendant in the years before it was written (when every petty German prince was said to be creating his own miniature Versailles) and England was alone among the constitutionalist states in not showing conspicuous signs of weakness. The decline of Venice into a torpor of corruption was a commonplace (*P.W.* ii. 14). The elective monarchy of Poland was a continual prey to internal factionalism and external interference. Elections to the Crown were occasions for venality and competition between rival foreign-influenced pressure groups. But an even more instructive example of the weakness of constitutionalism was available nearer to England than Poland or Venice.

Sir William Temple had excellent opportunities to observe the weaknesses of the Dutch machinery of government, for his successful negotiation of the Triple Alliance in 1668 had been in the teeth of constitutional forms.[23] The lesson was enforced by a second event with a less happy outcome, the collapse of the Dutch government under the pressure of the successful French invasion of 1672. The former Grand Pensionary, De Witt, who had been a particular friend of Temple's, was murdered in the streets of The Hague. In 1673 Temple published his first book, *Observations upon the United Provinces of the Netherlands*. In Chapter viii Temple offers an analysis of 'The Causes of their Fall in 1672'. His main criticisms of the Dutch are three: their failure to create an effective militia force and their consequent reliance on mercenaries, their lack of an effective head of state (there was no Stadtholder at this time), and the factional intrigues of the anti-Orangist party. 'A great Body' Temple describes

---

[22] *Letters*, ed. Frederick Bracher (Berkeley, 1974); there are frequent references to inactivity and to petty squabbles over ceremonial details.

[23] Homer E. Woodbridge, *Sir William Temple* (New York, 1940), pp. 80–93.

the Provinces, 'but without their usual Soul'.[24] Temple's analysis was, first of all, simple propaganda on behalf of William III, who at the point of crisis had assumed the stadt-holderate and saved the nation. But more generally, Temple's analysis was applicable to England. It too lacked an effective militia force; it was without a strong and impressive head of state capable of giving a lead to the nation; and it was a prey to factions. The analysis was also partially applicable to Poland (which had, however, a semi-effective militia). Characteristically enough in view of his belief in the role of climate and accident, Temple added to the reasons already given for the Dutch collapse a drought in early summer, 'an accident un-usual to their Climate'.[25] The drought was a chance occurrence, unique to the events of 1672. But the other causes of the Dutch collapse that Temple analyses had a general relevance. The closeness of Swift's political thought to Temple's is illustrated by the way in which we find these ideas mirrored in *Gulliver's Travels*. Brobdingnag is faction-free, has an impressive head of state, and an effective militia. Lilliput, by contrast, is ruled by the monarch of a party, is rent by factions, and has a standing army.

William III, the hero of the Dutch in 1672, played a similar role in England in 1688-9 and was hailed as the nation's deliverer. Yet he soon suffered a loss of his initial popularity in England. In part this was a natural reaction to a period of unnatural national unanimity. Men who agreed on nothing else agreed on being well rid of James. But as soon as the immediate crisis passed, and the problem of regularizing the constitution appeared, this unanimity was lost. Yet in the longer term William's loss of popularity had a basis in certain unforeseen consequences of the Revolution, particularly the expensive involvement in two decades of large-scale continental wars.[26]

Few Englishmen wanted to go back on the Revolution. The evils it had averted had been real enough. Where they

[24] *Observations*, ed. Clark, p. 139. The second quotation is also from p. 139.
[25] For the effects of the weather on the events of 1672, see Stephen B. Baxter, *William III* (London, 1966), pp. 64–6.
[26] It should be noted that this and the following account of English history since the Revolution represents Swift's point of view, not an objective analysis.

were seriously divided was in the degree of welcome they accorded it. Swift's attitude was cautiously conservative. In his 'Letter to Pope' (1721) Swift set out his considered attitude:

As to what is called a Revolution-principle, my opinion was this; That, whenever those evils which usually attend and follow a violent change of government, were not in probability so pernicious as the grievances we suffer under a present power, then the publick good will justify such a Revolution; and this I took to have been the Case in the Prince of Orange's expedition, although in the consequences it produced some very bad effects, which are likely to stick long enough by us. (*P.W.* ix.31.)

Swift's critique of contemporary society was based on his analysis of these 'very bad effects'.

In November 1710 Swift took over the editorship of the *Examiner*, a weekly paper written in support of the new Tory government. In the first number that he wrote (no. 13, 2 November) he offered his readers an analysis of what he was later to call the 'very bad effects' of the Revolution. The root of the problem, as Swift (applying Harringtonian principles) saw it, was the massive transfer of property (and, therefore, power) that had taken place: away from its original and rightful possessors, the landed gentry, to a new class of 'moneyed' men. This transfer had resulted in a minor social revolution, with Swift noting disapprovingly that too many of the smart new carriages that he saw about town were owned by military or moneyed men (*P.W.* iii. 5). But more important than the social were the constitutional changes. The Whigs had persuaded William III to cultivate a wrong interest—principally themselves, the moneyed men, and the dissenters—to the exclusion of the body of men who were the natural advisers and supports of the Crown, the men of substantial landed estates. The presence of the wrong men in parliament and in the royal councils had led to the manipulation of public finances for private advantages. Notions of good national housekeeping had been replaced by mysterious ideas of 'credit' and, most perniciously, by the absurd theory that it was to the nation's advantage to be in debt.[27]

---

[27] Thus the King of Brobdingnag was 'at a Loss how a Kingdom could run out of its Estate like a private Person. He asked me, who were our Creditors? and, where we found Money to pay them?' (II. vi. 131). For the rise of credit and the

Swift's analysis was partisan, calculated to appeal to the gentry on whom the ministry relied for its support in parliament. But it was not the less genuinely felt for that. If we look for similar sentiments expressed by the Tory leaders, we find them coming not from Oxford (who remained at heart a 'manager' rather than a party leader) but from Bolingbroke, who (with whatever sincerity) posed as a spokesman for the tax-oppressed gentry. Writing to the Earl of Orrery in 1709, his analysis was the same as Swift's:

We have been twenty years engaged in the two most expensive wars that Europe ever saw. The whole burthen of this charge has lain upon the landed interest during the whole time . . . A new interest has been created out of their fortunes, and a sort of property, which was not known twenty years ago, is now encreased to be almost equal to the terra firma of our island.[28]

He expressed the same sentiments in the *Letter to Sir William Wyndham* that he wrote in 1717 (it was not published until 1753) as a political apologia: 'The proprietor of the land, and the merchant who brought riches home by the returns of foreign trade, had during two wars bore the whole immense load of the national expenses; whilst the lender of money, who added nothing to the common stock, throve by the public calamity, and contributed not a mite to the public charge.'[29] Bolingbroke's 'politics of nostalgia' (as they have been called) found a convinced exponent in Swift.[30]

Of course, neither Swift nor Bolingbroke supposed that the Revolution was the source of all the country's ills. The sudden change in the government and the following wars had merely speeded up a process that had been going on for centuries: the gradual transfer of power through property. What was dramatic and distasteful to them about the post-Revolution rise of the moneyed men was that power had been transferred too fast, and to the wrong people. Like most of

---

'moneyed interest', in this period, see P. G. M. Dickson, *The Financial Revolution in England* (London, 1967).

[28] 'Letters of Henry St. John to the Earl of Orrery 1709-11', ed. H. T. Dickinson, *Camden Miscellany*, xxvi (London, 1975), p. 146.

[29] *Works*, ed. David Mallet (London, 1754), i. 11.

[30] Isaac Kramnick, *Bolingbroke and His Circle: The Politics of Nostalgia in the Age of Walpole* (Cambridge, Mass., 1968). On Swift in particular, see pp. 206-17.

his contemporaries, Swift believed in a constitution that balanced the powers of prince, nobles, and people. He was inclined to locate the closest that England had come to achieving this ideal balance in the reign of Elizabeth I (*P.W.* i. 230). But the continual alienation of Crown lands had destroyed this balance and finally left the crown too weak financially to resist the encroachments of the nobles and people. The result was the civil war in the mid-seventeenth century and the permanently weakened power of the royal prerogative (*P.W.* ix. 220). To the extent that the Revolution had curbed James II's attempt to revive the prerogative, it had been welcome. But to the extent that, instead of confirming power in the hands of the men of landed property, it had set up a factitious moneyed interest, its effects were to be deplored and if possible reversed. Since the Revolution, the Crown had been permanently dependent on parliament for regular supplies of money. Its ability to give a lead in national policy was correspondingly diminished. The prestige of the monarchy also suffered from the interruption to the hereditary principle. No sovereign during Swift's maturity enjoyed an undisputed title.

The vacuum left by this contraction of royal power and prestige had been filled in undesirable ways: by parties, by 'juntos' of ministers, by 'prime' ministers. By controlling the means of supply, such sinister forces were able to dictate to, or at least to impose some sort of terms on, the monarch. The Crown had become the prisoner of unscrupulous factional interests. Almost everyone deplored parties and their effects on the political health of the nation. It was with a rare candour that Bolingbroke admitted, 'I am afraid that we came to court in the same dispositions as all parties have done; that the principal spring of our actions was to have the government of the state in our hands; that our principal views were the conservation of this power, great employments to our selves, and great opportunities of rewarding those who had helped to raise us, and of hurting those who stood in opposition to us.'[31] For the typical attitude was to deplore parties while identifying one's own party with the nation as a

[31] *Works*, ed. Mallet, i. 8-9.

whole. This was Swift's publicly expressed position in 1710–14. Thus in the *Examiner* no. 31 (8 March 1711) he concluded his 'Fable of Faction' by confining the term 'faction' to 'those who set themselves up against the true Interest and Constitution of their Country' (i.e. the Whigs) and denying it to 'so great and unforced a Majority, with the QUEEN at the Head' as the Tories (*P.W.* iii. 103–4). By 1726 'party' had become a party issue, with the Tories generally arguing that the old party labels had lost their significance and the Whigs insisting on their continuing relevance. So one should probably not make too much of the fact that, in Lilliput, there is little to choose between the parties.

Even more sinister and reprehensible was the power of the leaders who manipulated party for personal advantage, as Swift accused the Whig leaders of doing. Swift's ideal was that individuals should be prepared to serve the Crown as the Crown's personal servants, not as part of some party deal. Thus in the *Examiner* he particularly criticizes the first movements towards cabinet solidarity whereby the Whigs had defeated Harley's attempted palace revolution in 1708 and tried to frustrate his take-over of the government in 1710. Nothing, in Swift's view, could be more absurd or improper than for ministers to bargain with the Crown about the conditions on which they would accept employment: '*Madam, I cannot serve you while such a One is in Employment. I desire humbly to resign my Commission, if Mr. . . . continues Secretary of State*' (*P.W.* iii. 37). Swift would have liked a scheme like Temple's reformed Privy Council of 1679 to operate again: genuine collective advice and responsibility instead of factional domination of decision-making.[32]

Most sinister of all was the development of the office of a 'prime minister', in Swift's day and after a term more often of abuse than of respect.[33] Swift disapproved strongly of the

---

[32] Woodbridge, *Sir William Temple*, pp. 193–6; see above, p. 28, n. 42.

[33] Although in the *Proposal for Correcting the English Tongue* Swift used the title to compliment Oxford (*P.W.* iv. 17). Perhaps he felt that Queen Anne's weakness made the office a temporary necessity. Soon after the Restoration, when Ormonde suggested to Clarendon that he should become 'prime minister', Clarendon replied that he would rather be hanged than accept such a position, having previously advised Charles II that '*England* would not bear a Favourite, nor any one Man, who should out of his Ambition engross to himself the Disposal of the

way in which Walpole was supposed to be running the whole
governmental machine of the country for the sole benefit of
himself, his family, and his cronies. His clearest indictment
(outside *Gulliver's Travels* itself) of the office of prime minister is in the unfinished 'Account of the Court and Empire
of Japan', which he wrote about 1728 but which was not
published until 1765. The 'Account' is an allegory of English
history from the reign of Queen Anne until the accession of
George II in 1727. The office of prime minister is clearly
associated with eastern despotism. Lelop-Aw (Walpole) speaks
of the 'laudable custom of all Eastern princes, to leave the
whole management of affairs, both civil and military, to their
Visirs' (*P.W.* v. 106). The 'Account' unfortunately breaks off
with Lelop-Aw's speech in praise of his own methods, arguing
that 'without this bribery and corruption, the wheels of
government will not turn' (*P.W.* v. 106). Royal favourites had
been one of the hazards of government throughout history.
What seemed sinister about the office of a 'prime minister' in
contemporary England was not just that it smacked of absolutism and despotism but that in modern parliamentary
conditions a prime minister might enjoy security of tenure
through controlling the royal purse strings. With the Crown
in his pocket, there was no power able to prevent him en-
riching himself with the spoils of the nation.

In retrospect, the last four years of the reign of Queen Anne
came to appear to Swift as an oasis in the midst of two deserts
of Whig rule. He forgot the daily frustrations that had been
caused by the procrastinations of Oxford and the paralysis
created by the power struggle between Oxford and Bolingbroke. For whatever the faults of those ministers had been,
they were negligible when set against the embodied corruption
of the Whig administrations under George I.[34] Swift was
prepared to believe any evil of these Whig governments. It
went without saying that they were corrupt, that ministers
enriched themselves at the public expense. One major scandal

---

publick Affairs'; *The Life of Edward, Earl of Clarendon* (Oxford, 1759; octavo
edition), ii. 88.

[34] The real George I was not the monster seen by Swift's prejudiced eyes.
For a sympathetic portrait of George as an enlightened and far from despotic
figure, see Ragnhild Hatton, *George I: Elector and King* (London, 1978).

was the South Sea Bubble of 1720 in which government ministers and the king's mistress certainly, and possibly the king
himself, were involved. A later and smaller-scale scandal, but
one with which Swift himself was particularly concerned, was
the grant in 1722 of a patent to William Wood to mint a new
copper coinage for Ireland. Wood had obtained the patent
through a bribe to the king's mistress, the Duchess of Kendal.
Thus the Whig government and the court were certainly not
above reproach. But on some questions Swift's opinions
merely reflect his political partisanship: for example, his
attitude to the government's treatment of the prisoners taken
after the failure of the 1715 rebellion. By any impartial
account, the government acted with moderation and human-
ity. Yet Swift could compare its handling of the 1715 rebellion with Jeffereys's treatment of Monmouth's rebels under
James II (*P.W.* v. 284).[35]

Swift's dislike of George I is well known and certainly
found expression in *Gulliver's Travels*. But it would give a
one-sided impression to end this account of his attitude to
contemporary politics on an unreservedly gloomy note. There
were men, even in modern times, whom Swift admired: men
like Sir William Temple. Among monarchs the foremost in
Swift's estimation was Charles XII of Sweden. Swift's admiration for Charles XII has been to a large extent overlooked,
and repays closer attention. Although he did not make a contribution so direct as George I's to *Gulliver's Travels*, the
grounds on which Swift admired him help to illustrate Swift's
political values and the background of thought that created
Gulliver.

Swift had two very important personal sources of information about Sweden, and it is noteworthy that both were
highly favourable to Charles XII. The first was John Robinson,
the cleric and diplomat whom Oxford promoted to the
bishopric of London.[36] Robinson wrote an *Account of Sueden*
(1694) not unlike Temple's *Observations upon the United*

---

[35] It should be noted, however, that some historians offer assessments of the
Walpole régime hardly less damning than Swift's; see, in particular, E. P. Thompson,
Whigs and Hunters (New York, 1975), especially pp. 197–202.
[36] R. M. Hatton, 'John Robinson and the *Account of Sueden*', *Bulletin of the
Institute of Historical Research*, xxviii (1955), 128–59.

Provinces. His long residence in Sweden gave him a natural sympathy for the country and its king. During the War of the Spanish Succession he was frequently called upon when an envoy was needed who could speak Swedish and who enjoyed the confidence of Charles XII. In 1707 Marlborough wrote to Godolphin that Charles having 'a particular confidence in the integrity of Mr. Robinson and of his knowledge of those matters would be glad he might be employed by the Queen'.[37] Later Robinson's known pro-Swedish sympathies made Godolphin unwilling to use him in negotiations involving Charles's enemy, Augustus II of Poland.[38] Swift's second important source was Count Gyllenborg, Swedish Resident in London at the time of Swift's residence there in 1710-14. Gyllenborg was a sympathizer with the Tories and later an intriguer with the Jacobites: in 1717 a major scandal was caused as the result of his arrest (in violation of usual diplomatic immunity) in connection with the Swedo-Jacobite invasion scare.[39] Memories of the occasion no doubt played a part in the genesis of Gulliver's discourse on plots at the Academy of Lagado (III. vi. 190-2).

It was the death of Charles XII in 1718 that evoked the most important surviving pieces of evidence of Swift's admiration for him. 'I am personally concerned for the Death of the K of Sweden', he wrote in a letter to Charles Ford on 6 January 1719, 'because I intended to have beggd my Bread at His Court, whenever our good Friends in Power thought fit to put me and my Brethren under the necessity of begging. Besides I intended him an honor and a Compliment, which I never yet thought a Crownd head worth, I mean, dedicating a Book to him' (*Corr.* ii. 311).[40] (Swift had perhaps forgotten, or did not count as his own, his dedication of Temple's

---

[37] *The Marlborough–Godolphin Correspondence*, ed. Henry L. Snyder (Oxford, 1975), ii. 759.

[38] *The Marlborough–Godolphin Correspondence*, iii. 1367.

[39] For a detailed account, see J. F. Chance, 'The "Swedish Plot" of 1716-17', *English Historical Review*, xvii (1903), 81-106.

[40] Another piece of evidence of Swift's admiration for Charles XII is a manuscript, once owned by him, which contains a Latin prose character of Charles (written by a Polish nobleman) and a short Latin poem on Charles's defeat at Poltava. The prose character is eulogistic, praising Charles's martial prowess, piety, liberality, modesty, and other virtues. The manuscript is now in the Henry E. Huntington Library, San Marino (HM 14366).

Letters to William III in 1700.) The work Swift intended to
have dedicated to Charles was a 'History of England' of the
kind that Temple had planned and begun but not taken
beyond the reign of William I. Swift seems to have had the
project in contemplation since at least 1703 (*P.W.* v. 11),
although in the event it was never much advanced. In 1719,
however, Swift's interest in the work revived sufficiently for
him to write a dedication, not of course to the late king but
to Count Gyllenborg. It is not clear exactly what the impulse
to take the work off the shelf was, but it may reasonably be
connected with the general revival of interest in the outside
world that later led Swift to intervention in Irish politics and
to the composition of *Gulliver's Travels*. Swift wrote in the
dedication:

My intention was to inscribe it to the king your late master, for whose
great virtues I had ever the highest veneration, as I shall continue to
bear to his memory . . . when I looked round on all the princes of
Europe, I could think of none who might deserve that distinction for
me, besides the king your master . . . neither can I be suspected of
flattery on this point, since it was some years after that I had the
honour of an invitation to his court . . . which I heartily repent that
I did not accept.   (*P.W.* v. 11.)

There is another tantalizing glimpse of Swift's relations with
Charles XII in a letter Pope wrote to Arbuthnot after visiting
Swift at Letcombe Basset in 1714. Swift 'talked of Politicks
over Coffee, with the Air and Style of an old Statesman' and
'gave us a Hint as if he had a Correspondence with the King
of Sweden'.[41]
      At first sight it may appear strange that Swift should con-
sider dedicating an English history to Charles XII or one of
his former ministers. Sir Harold Williams called it 'a curious
choice in either instance' (*Corr*. iii. 63). But the apparent
puzzle is readily explicable in political terms. Between the
return to Sweden of Charles XII in 1714 and his death in
1718, he and George I were the two great rival kings of
western Europe. Louis XIV was inactive, and died in 1715;
Louis XV was a child at his accession. The other monarchs
were lesser figures, with the exception of Peter the Great of

      [41] Pope, *Correspondence*, ed. George Sherburn (Oxford, 1956), i. 234.

Russia who can hardly be considered a western figure. In 1719, one of the most obvious indirect ways to register one's disapproval of George I was to praise Charles XII. If Swift had completed and published his history at that time, the dedication to Gyllenborg would have been a flagrant act of political partisanship, a scarcely veiled snub to George I. Swift had written: 'when I looked round on all the princes of *Europe*, I could think of none who might deserve that distinction [a dedication] from me, besides the king your master; (for I say nothing of his present *Britannick* majesty, to whose person and character I am an utter stranger, and like to continue so)' (*P.W.* v. 11). More generally, Charles XII and George I represented contrasting styles of kingship. It would be wrong to suggest that when, in Part I of *Gulliver's Travels*, Swift drew a contrast between the ambitious tyranny of the Emperor of Lilliput and the more gracious behaviour of the Emperor of Blefuscu, he was thinking of this contrast between George I and Charles XII. The satire in *Gulliver* is not so specific as that. But the contrast between the two kings was an important factor in his attitude to monarchy, and informs the treatment of it in *Gulliver's Travels*.

Charles himself was in his time and has remained to historians an enigmatic figure. Contemporaries tended to view him selectively, picking out those traits in his complex and elusive personality that fitted their picture of him. Even today, it is not easy to arrive at an objective estimate.[42] The first point to note in connection with Charles and Swift is that English attitudes to Charles were strongly coloured by party prejudice. He was always popular with the Tories and disliked by the Whigs, before 1709 for his failure to join the alliance against France and after 1714 as a supporter of the Jacobites and the principal stumbling-block to George I's ambitions to enlarge his electorate with parts of the disintegrating Swedish empire. Yet it would be wrong to see Swift's admiration for Charles as solely or even mainly dictated by party prejudice. For in many ways Charles was an embodiment of those 'old' virtues that Swift found so attractive. We can see this aspect of Charles in a letter that

---

[42] The following account is largely based on R. M. Hatton, *Charles XII of Sweden* (London, 1968); cited in the text as Hatton.

John Robinson wrote to a diplomatic superior in 1700. Robinson stressed the king's piety, liberality, self-control, courage and endurance, and frugality:

His Maj^ty is known to be very regular in his private devotions . . . treats Religion with much respect, yet free from any superstitious observances . . . He is liberal in the highest degree, much more a Master of the Passion of Anger, than his prededess^ors have ordinarily been; very just in his Sentiments, and of great clemency . . . His Courage and intrepidity have not yet the bounds they reasonably ought . . . He affects to appear more like a Soldier than a Courtier, goes plain in his Cloaths, is yet more indifferent as to his Diet, and very rarely drinks any Wine. He is perhaps the most indefatigable person in His Kingdom, sleeps little, and on the ground or a bench as well as abed . . . His thoughts are much taken up with the prospect of doing great things.[43]

This is much the same cluster of virtues as Swift evokes in the picture in *Gulliver's Travels* of 'some *English* Yeomen of the old Stamp . . . once so famous for the Simplicity of their Manners, Dyet and Dress; for Justice in their Dealings; for their true Spirit of Liberty; for their Valour and Love of their Country' (III. viii. 201).

Charles's piety was of the simple non-polemical kind that Swift prized above minute theological enquiry (the implied contrast in Robinson's letter is obviously with the priest-ridden James II). When another and less sympathetic English diplomat, Lord Raby (later, as Earl of Strafford, plenipotentiary at Utrecht), visited Charles at his headquarters in Saxony in 1707, he stressed the squalor in which Charles habitually lived, with the single exception of 'a fine gilt Bible by His Bedside, the only thing that looks fine in all his Equipage'.[44] The Bible was not for show, for Charles was

[43] John Robinson to Sir Charles Hedges, 22 December 1970 N.S. British Library, Add. MS 41178, ff. 135–6. Subsequent quotations from Robinson are from this letter.

[44] 'A Character of Charles 12th K: of Sweden in a Letter from Lord Raby to Lord Halifax in 1707'. British Library, Add. MS 35885, ff. 1–4. Subsequent quotations from Raby are from this letter. Despite his later service under the Tory government and impeachment by the Whigs, Raby was not a Tory. In *British Politics in the Age of Anne* (London, 1967), Geoffrey Holmes calls him 'the most persistent and shameless go-getter of his day' to whom it would be 'quite irrelevant to attach a party tag' (p. 386). His letter to Halifax typifies the Whig attitude to Charles. Writing to Halifax (a prominent Whig) Raby would naturally write what he thought Halifax would want to hear (I owe this suggestion to Professor Stephen B. Baxter).

known to read in it every day (Hatton, pp. 341-2). The comparison of the reports of the two diplomats is instructive, for it shows the same qualities through the eyes of a sympathetic and an unfriendly witness. Where Robinson had described Charles as 'indifferent as to his Diet', Raby obviously found Charles's Spartan table manners more than he could stomach: 'Between every bit of meat he eats a piece of bread and butter, which He spreads with his thumbs'. Similarly, where Robinson had spoken of Charles as 'plain in his Cloaths', Raby refers to his 'old leathern waistcoat and breeches, which they tell me are sometimes so greasy, that they may be fry^d'.

Charles was personally chaste, and disapproved of incontinence in others. In his strict attitude to adultery he refused to make exceptions for those he called 'royal whores' (Hatton, p. 179). Here was a striking contrast with George I. On campaign Charles shared the hardships and privations of his own soldiers. His personal courage, indeed, was even excessive for a king-general, and Robinson struck a prophetic note when he spoke of Charles's intrepidity as having 'putt His Relations and Subjects into perpetual fears, that he would one day fall ingloriously . . . nothing being sufficient to persuade Him to any tolerable degree of care for His safety'. These fears were justified by Charles's death at Frederickshald in 1718.

Charles's fearlessness was not his only double-edged quality. Robinson reported him 'almost unalterably firm in his Resolutions once taken'. This could often be a liability, especially in negotiations which required flexibility. Thus Bolingbroke, anxious for his own purposes to save Charles and Sweden from disaster, lamented to Matthew Prior in 1714 that 'the inflexible obstinacy which this Prince has shewn, and the high terms he has insisted upon, even at the lowest ebb of his fortune, have made it impossible for his true friends to speak and act in his behalfe, as they might on several occasions have done with great probability of success'.[45]

Yet Charles was not a mere military man. He had a wide range of intellectual interests, including music, mathematics, and architecture. These were most in evidence during his stay

---

[45] Bolingbroke to Prior, 6 May 1714; *British Diplomatic Instructions 1689–1789: ii, France 1689–1721*, ed. L. G. Wickham Legg (London, 1925; Camden Society, 3rd series, vol. xxxv), p. 68.

in Lund in 1716–18. At the same period Charles showed an interest in speculative theology, but he carefully refrained from publishing some defences of certain theses that might have been suspected of unorthodoxy (Hatton, pp. 428–32). The image of the warrior-king passing his leisure in a university town, attending lectures and taking part in its intellectual life, is one that would strongly have appealed to Swift. It had Platonic resonances, while the idealized King of Brobdingnag is 'as learned a Person as any in his Dominions' (II. iii. 103). In 1715 the French diplomat, Croissy, reported home to his minister, Torcy, that 'Sa conversation est tres aimable, je me sens a mon aise avec luy et je crois pour lors entretenir plutôt un Philosophe qu'un Roy'.[46] Of particular appeal to Swift, in view of his own interest in an academy to guard the purity of English, would have been Charles's interest in the Swedish language, his concern to preserve its purity, to replace unnecessary loan words by Swedish coinages, and to make it a fit instrument for the subtlest thought and the most complex arguments (Hatton, pp. 13, 217, 432). With all these qualities of Charles's, Swift might have shared the opinion of some of the king's own intimates that he was an able peace-time monarch forced by adverse circumstances into almost perpetual war.

Charles was an absolute king, and Swift was a convinced opponent of absolutism. Yet Swift also shared Sir William Temple's belief in the determining effect a monarch's character might have on his country's destiny. Plato, too, had envisaged the possibility of shortcutting the need to educate a whole society to virtue by so educating its prince. With Dionysius the younger he even tried to put this idea into practice. Thus it was possible for Swift to suppose that absolute power might, on occasion, be more properly lodged in the hands of a philosopher-king than in the hands of a corrupt ministry or a selfish aristocracy. Such ideas were later to find philosophical elaboration in Bolingbroke's *The Idea of a Patriot King* (written about 1738, although not published until 1749). Swift knew that the Swedish monarchy had been limited and elective until Charles XI had made it hereditary

---

[46] Croissy to Torcy, 27 May 1715. Paris, Archives du Ministère des Affaires Étrangères, Correspondance Politique, Suède, vol. 132, ff. 83ᵛ–84ʳ.

and absolute in 1680-6. Yet sympathetic observers might view Charles XI's constitutional revolution in a favourable light as being primarily a curb on the exorbitant power of the nobility. Indeed, Charles's changes were facilitated by the support he received from the non-noble estates. Similarly, it was easy for Swift, with a Tory outlook on foreign affairs, to see Charles XII not as a modern Caesar or Alexander but almost as a Scipio or a Cato. 'He was the first that ever had the ambition to be a conqueror, without wishing to increase his dominions. His desire to gain kingdoms, was only that he might give them away'.[47] To Swift he appeared as a great liberator and defender of liberty. His first campaign, against Denmark in 1700, was fought on behalf of the Duke of Holstein–Gottorp against the encroachments of the tyrannous Frederick IV of Denmark. The duke was married to Charles's elder sister, and Swedish policy had long been to use the alliance as a means of putting pressure on Denmark from the rear. But despite this dynastic element, a sympathetic observer could see Charles as primarily a protector of the weak against the oppression of a more powerful neighbour. Charles's next campaign, against Poland, was also waged on impeccable moral grounds. Charles accused Augustus II of having invaded Swedish Livonia and of having disregarded traditional Polish liberties in an attempt to establish a despotic state. Swift himself had no love for German princes who acquired other realms which they then proceeded to exploit for selfish dynatic advantage. Augustus, as Elector of Saxony, had used his Saxon troops to threaten the Polish constitution. After 1714, George I (in the Tory interpretation of events) did almost exactly the same, or at least would have liked to have done. The comparison was exploited by Atterbury in a pamphlet, violently anti-Whig and anti-Hanoverian, that he wrote to infuse life into the Tory election campaign in 1715: 'The *Polish* Subjects of King *Augustus* were indeed free, when they chose him, from being an *Elector* of the Empire, and of a different Religion from theirs, to be their King; but he being confined to certain Conditions, which he did not like, soon

[47] Voltaire, *The History of Charles XII King of Sweden* (London, 1732), Book VIII, p. 170. Swift owned a copy of this translation (no. 413 in the sale catalogue). Raby's letter to Halifax (n. 44 above) is printed in an appendix.

found Means to break them'.[48] The particular reference is to
the limitations placed on George by the Act of Settlement.
So as not to lose any point in the implied comparison, Atterbury was at pains to point out that George's Lutheranism was
closer to Catholicism than to Anglicanism (p. 20). Swift, like
Atterbury, would have been sympathetic to Charles fighting
the ambitions of a German prince out to aggrandize himself.

Charles's catastrophic defeat at Poltava, paradoxically
enough, could only have endeared him further to Swift.
Charles's defeat could be attributed to the accidental wound
in his foot that had prevented him from commanding in person (thus illustrating Temple's *maxima e minimis* theory).[49]
Swift, as we have seen, particularly admired noble failures.
'Victrix causa deis placuit, sed victa Catoni'. Swift had always
been on the side of Cato, not the gods. His regard for Charles
would have been further strengthened by the latter's direct
opposition, after his return from Turkey in 1714, to the
ambitions of his former ally George I. Swift had a particular
dislike for political ingratitude: it looms large in his treatment
of the allies in *The Conduct of the Allies* (1711), and in the
politics of Lilliput (I. vii. 73). George had once been Sweden's
ally, but had deserted it for selfish motives: to add the
Swedish possessions of Bremen and Verden to Hanover.[50]
George needed to use British resources to secure this objective, in defiance of the spirit of the Act of Settlement.
Gulliver ironically tells his Houyhnhnm master that 'it is
justifiable to enter into a War against our nearest Ally, when
one of his Towns lies convenient for us, or a Territory of
Land, that would render our Dominions round and compact'
(IV. v. 246). This is surely a glance at George's relations with
Sweden. The king and his Whig ministers played an underhand
game to secure the necessary parliamentary consent and
supplies for British naval expeditions to the Baltic, nominally
to protect British trade but really to further George's northern

[48] *English Advice to the Freeholders of England* (London, 1714), p. 17.
Although dated 1714 on the title-page, the pamphlet was actually published
early in January 1715. For the circumstances, see G. V. Bennett, *The Tory Crisis
in Church and State* (Oxford, 1975), pp. 192–4.

[49] See above, pp. 27, 30.

[50] John J. Murray, *George I, the Baltic, and the Whig Split* (London, 1969),
p. 57.

ambitions. One incident in this game was the exposure, at precisely the moment best calculated to influence parliament, of the 'plot' which Gyllenborg had been concerting with the English Jacobites. It was such expedients that were in Swift's mind when Gulliver speaks of the usefulness of plots 'to restore new Vigour to a crazy Administration; to stifle or divert general Discontents' (III. vi. 191). He would later see the arrest and trial of Atterbury as another cynical move by the Whig government to deflect attention away from ministerial corruption and incompetence. In the case of the Gyllenborg affair, the government's actions were additionally reprehensible as designed to buy the support of the king by toadying to his expansionist aims for his electorate.

The character and career of Charles XII provide perfect illustrations of the kind of lessons that Swift drew from history, lessons supportive of his generally pessimistic political philosophy. Charles, a noble and wise philosopher-king, forced by circumstances to engage in an incessant fight to preserve his own lands (though still willing to fight for the cause of liberty elsewhere), had been defeated by accidents, by treachery and ingratitude, and by the petty intrigues of lesser and more selfish men. Such Swift knew to be the probable fate of latter-day heroes who had the misfortune to live in the squalid world of contemporary political intrigue. By the time he came to write *Gulliver's Travels* in 1721–5, his temperamental bias towards pessimism had been deepened and reinforced by his own experiences and by an admittedly selective reading of history. Together these factors made for rather a jaundiced perspective on the contemporary scene, but biased as they are it is through them that we must approach the politics of *Gulliver's Travels*.

CHAPTER 3

Motte and Faulkner

The interpretation of the politics of *Gulliver's Travels* is bound up with certain textual problems. For two substantive editions of the work were published in Swift's lifetime, differing in usually small but sometimes important ways. The differences of substance involve only a few passages, but (and this is no accident) several are of major political significance. The changes made in the later text are in the direction of making the political satire more explicit, and there are enough of them to affect the way in which readers approach the work as a whole. Thus their cumulative effect is greater than the sum of the effects of the individual changes. Some attention to the textual problem is therefore a necessary preliminary to an interpretation of *Gulliver*'s politics.[1]

Gulliver's Travels was first published in London by Benjamin Motte on 28 October 1726. Swift neither supervised the printing of this edition nor corrected proof. The publication of the work was handled anonymously and through intermediaries. After publication he complained of the book's 'mangled and murdered Pages' (*Corr.* iv. 197–8). A second substantive text appeared as Volume III of a four-volume edition of Swift's *Works* published by George Faulkner (Dublin, 1735). Although he stopped short of acknowledging this to be the authorised edition we now know it was, Swift did allow Faulkner to claim the authority of 'an intimate Friend of the Author's' for the text of *Gulliver's Travels* (*Corr.* v. 263). The respective merits of these two major editions of Swift's masterpiece have been the subject of a long scholarly controversy. The case for the superiority of Faulkner's text was cogently put by Sir Harold Williams; the brief for Motte was

---

[1] I have, however, ignored textual questions (such as the extent to which Swift was responsible for the minor variants in Faulkner's edition) which have no bearing on the book's politics. Motte published three editions of *Gulliver's Travels* in 1726; but the variants do not affect the meaning.

taken by Arthur E. Case.[2] There is no need to rehearse their arguments, for Williams's conclusions have won general acceptance and Faulkner's text is now regarded as the more authoritative. Most modern editions and reprints with any pretensions to accuracy of text are based on it, as is the standard edition of *Gulliver's Travels* in Herbert Davis's edition of Swift's *Prose Writings* (*P.W.* xi).

In reopening the question, and arguing in favour of a re-valuation of Motte's text of the *Travels*, I am not trying to revive the arguments used by Case. In the terms in which he and Williams disagreed, the question has been settled in William's favour. But two of the assumptions on which they both worked need to be examined. The first is whether Motte really tampered with the text of *Gulliver's Travels* as Swift claimed he did. Everyone has taken Swift's word for this, despite his notorious unreliability (to use no stronger word) on the subject of the publication of his works and his responsibility for them. The second is whether there may not be a case for preferring what Swift originally wrote to a revised text, even where the revised readings are definitely attribut-able to the author. For when Williams and Case wrote, it was accepted as axiomatic that an editor must accept an author's revisions of his own work. Greg, for example, thought that even a 'presumed' revision should be 'admitted into the text, whether the editor himself considers it an improvement or not'.[3] This is no longer generally accepted. James Thorpe has written convincingly and at length about textual problems in which an editor is squarely faced with an aesthetic choice between what Thorpe prefers to call 'versions' rather than texts of a literary work.[4] The Motte and Faulkner editions of *Gulliver's Travels* are really 'versions' in this sense. Swift's intentions changed between 1726 and 1735, and each text represents his intention at the time. Neither can be regarded as more authoritative than the other. If we want Swift's last

[2] *Gulliver's Travels*, ed. Harold Williams (London, 1926), Introduction; Williams, *The Text of 'Gulliver's Travels'* (Cambridge, 1952); Case, 'The Text of *Gulliver's Travels'*, *Four Essays on 'Gulliver's Travels'* (Princeton, 1945), pp. 1–49.

[3] 'The Rationale of Copy-Text' (1949), *Collected Papers*, ed. J. C. Maxwell (Oxford, 1966), p. 387.

[4] *Principles of Textual Criticism* (San Marino, 1972), especially pp. 32–49.

thoughts, we will turn to the 1735 text; if we are interested in *Gulliver's Travels* as he originally wrote it and as it made an impact on its first audience of 1726, we will turn instead to Motte's edition.

This relationship between the two versions has hitherto been obscured by taking too seriously Swift's abuse of Motte's printing of the text. Careful examination of the evidence, as I shall show in detail later, vindicates the integrity of Motte's edition as a faithful representation of what Swift wrote. Clearing Motte from Swift's facetious aspersions allows the two versions to be compared on a more equal basis than has previously been the case. What such comparison reveals is that in most cases Swift's second thoughts, in matters of substance rather than style, were out of harmony with his original conception of the work. This is consistent with what other evidence we have about the pre-publication history of *Gulliver's Travels*. The two questions, whether Motte tampered with the text and how Swift's conception of *Gulliver* altered, are mutually illuminating. More is involved than the vindication of Motte's professional integrity. A just view of the textual problem allows us to restore to *Gulliver's Travels* itself something of the original nobility of purpose that Swift himself later partially lost sight of.

Swift's intentions in writing *Gulliver's Travels* changed over the period of composition, publication, and revision. Since the whole process extended over fifteen years, there is nothing surprising in this. But as a result, the satire is not all of a piece. For much of the book Swift seems intent on a satire, unlimited in its application by time or place, on the nature of man, society, and political activity. Yet this satire is occasionally disfigured by temporary, topical, allusions and teasingly opaque allegories. These have provided material for annotators, but they hardly enhance *Gulliver* as a work of art. Pope, who faced the same problem in his poems, that of wanting to speak both to his contempories and to posterity, warned Swift of the dangers. Writing just a few weeks after the publication of *Gulliver's Travels*, he urged him 'if you must needs write about Politicks at all . . . surely it ought to be so as to preserve the dignity and integrity of your character with those times to come, which will most impartially judge of them' (*Corr.* iii. 182). This warning comes just after a reference to advances made to Swift by Daniel Pulteney, an opposition politician. Clearly Pope saw that there was as much danger to be feared from joining the opposition to Walpole as from any offers the government might make to buy Swift off. In general, Swift heeded the warning. He did not contribute to the *Craftsman*, as he was probably invited to do. But he had allowed *Gulliver's Travels* to contain a number of inappositely specific hits at the Walpole regime. And when he came to revise his masterpiece, instead of weeding them out he allowed a few more to creep in.

Swift's original impulse in writing *Gulliver's Travels* was certainly to create a general satire on the follies of European civilization as a whole, not just on the failings of contemporary English society. This European relevance was recognized by one of *Gulliver's* earliest critics. Abel Boyer noted that through various fictional strategies 'the Author characterizes several Princes and Nations of *Europe*'.[5] The earliest stages of composition are obscure, but we know from a letter of Swift's to Charles Ford that *Gulliver* was in progress by April 1721 (*Corr.* ii. 381). The work was thus begun when Swift was just coming out of a period of complete demoralization and disillusionment with political activity. It was at this time that he assured Pope that he was living 'in the greatest privacy, and utter ignorance of those events which are most commonly talked of in the world; I neither know the Names nor Number of the Family which now reigns, further than the Prayer-book informs me' (*Corr.* ii. 367). At this period of his life, if ever, Swift was able to stand above the party conflict. It was in this mood that the non-partisan satire on party politics in Lilliput was conceived.

This mood, and Swift's detachment, did not last. In January 1724 he wrote to Ford that 'I have left the Country of Horses, and am in the flying Island, where I shall not stay long, and my two last Journeys will be soon over' (*Corr.* iii. 5). By this time Swift was again politically active: his stand against Wood's halfpence in the *Drapier's Letters* (1724) committed him to total opposition to the Irish policy of the English Whig

---

[5] *Political State of Great Britain*, xxxii (December 1726), 461.

government. Ireland benefited, but *Gulliver's Travels* did not. Part III, written last, contains the most frequent references to the events of the 1720s. But more serious than a few occasional allusions is the loss of objectivity. This can be seen in the comparative treatment of politics in Lilliput and Laputa. There is little to chose between the Big-endians and the Little-endians or the High-heels and the Low-heels. But in Laputa, the king, his ministers, and the reigning philosophy have a monopoly of opprobium. All the virtues are concentrated in Munodi, whose integrity is guaranteed by being out of favour with the king and court. In 1726, the year in which *Gulliver's Travels* was finally revised and published, Swift returned to England for the first time since 1714. Once in England, he became caught up once more in English politics. He may have had hopes of finding preferment for himself; certainly he lent moral support to opposition politicians. Several passages in *Gulliver*, which there are reasons for believing to be late additions, reflect this renewed political commitment.

The clandestine comedy with which Swift surrounded the actual publication of *Gulliver* is well known. It was partly due to Swift's desire to preserve his anonymity and partly out of his love of a good joke. He was in England for several months in 1726, certainly long enough to have arranged for the printing and proof-reading of *Gulliver* under his own supervision. Instead he chose to open negotiations with a publisher pseudonymously, and then only a few days before his departure for Ireland.[6] There was nothing unusual, for Swift, in all this. He liked to surround his writings with mystery, and to pretend not to have been concerned in their publication. His intimates knew how seriously to take such protestations. Thus in February 1711 he wrote to Stella that 'Some bookseller has raked up every thing I writ, and published it t'other day in one volume; but I know nothing of it, 'twas without my knowledge or consent . . . Took pretends he knows nothing of it, but I doubt he is at the bottom' (*J.S.* i. 203). Stella cannot have taken this very seriously, for the previous October Swift had written 'Tooke is going on with

[6] For the circumstances of publication, see Williams, *The Text of 'Gulliver's Travels'*, pp. 4-21.

my *Miscellany*' (*J.S.* i. 62).[7] Much later, writing to Pope about the *Dunciad*, Swift looked forward to seeing the elaborate *Variorum* edition 'with all his pomp of preface, etc. and many complaints of spurious editions' (*Corr.* iii. 293). Pope, too, enjoyed this kind of joke, although (unlike Swift) he usually ended by acknowledging his works.

What is surprising is not that Swift disowned the text and publication of *Gulliver's Travels* but that scholars have taken his joke so seriously. No one has ever doubted that Swift wrote the book; but his complaints against Motte have some- how obtained greater credence. In correspondence with Pope, Gay, and Arbuthnot in the first months after *Gulliver* was published, Swift kept up a pretence of knowing nothing of the authorship and of detecting corruptions in the text. He wrote to Pope in November 1726:

I read the Book over and in the second volume observe several passages which appear to be patched and altered, and the style of a different sort (unless I am much mistaken) . . . if I were Gulliver's friend, I would desire all my acquaintance to give out that his copy was basely mangled, and abused, and added to, and blotted out by the printer; for so to me it seems, in the second volume particularly.   (*Corr.* iii. 189–90.)

Are we to take these protestations any more literally than the story (told in the same letter) of the Irish bishop who thought *Gulliver* 'full of improbable lies, and for his part, he hardly believed a word of it'? When he prefixed the 'Letter from Capt. Gulliver, to His Cousin Symson' to the 1735 edition of the *Travels*, Swift made Gulliver complain of editorial mangling and abuse (*P.W.* xi. 5). Yet few readers would now confuse the Gulliver of that letter with Swift himself. Similarly the references in Swift's letters should be taken as part of an elaborately Scriblerian jest.

Why would Motte mangle, abuse, add to, or blot out from the text of *Gulliver's Travels*? The usual reason given is fear of prosecution. Swift himself liked to think of the *Travels* as dangerous to publish. At least he affected to think so when

---

[7] Davis notes, in connection with the 1711 *Miscellanies*, that 'this manner of denying all responsibility for the publication of books, which has friends knew perfectly well had been planned and prepared by him with considerable care, became a habit of playful irony by which later biographers and editors have sometimes been and may still be deceived' (*P.W.* ii. xxxviii).

he wrote to Pope in 1725 that the book was 'intended for the press when the world shall deserve them, or rather when a Printer shall be found brave enough to venture his Eares' (*Corr*. iii. 102). Actually this was probably more a reflection of what Swift liked to believe was the Whig government's repressive censorship policy than of the real state of affairs. Much later, in 1733, Swift wrote to Ford that 'it was to avoyd offence, that Motte got those alterations and insertions to be made I suppose by Mr Took the Clergyman deceased' (*Corr*. iv. 211). It does not exactly inspire confidence in Swift's story that he should only 'suppose' the alterations to be the work of a conveniently deceased cleric. In 1735 Faulkner's Preface to his edition of Swift's *Works* keeps up the charade of Swift being only the 'supposed Author'. Faulkner claimed to be printing certain works which 'the general Opinion' had fixed on Swift 'whether truly or no we shall not presume to determine'.[8] Yet there can be no doubt that, whatever degree of attention Swift bestowed on the proofs of Faulkner's edition, he was responsible for its contents and exclusions. Swift's comments about the publication of his works simply cannot be taken at face value.

Was Swift's original manuscript, as it was supposedly 'dropp'd at his house in the dark, from a Hackney-coach' (*Corr*. iii. 181) and received by Motte, such as to make prosecution likely and therefore censorship by Motte or one of his agents prudent? It is impossible to be certain about this, but scholars have almost certainly overestimated the likelihood. Sir Charles Firth suggested that in Swift's time 'it was dangerous to write plainly about public affairs, or to criticize public men with any freedom'.[9] Most subsequent commentary on the problem has been based on an assumption of the accuracy of Firth's statement. But it needs, at the least, serious qualification. Phillip Harth notes that it 'would surely have come as a surprise to Walpole, forced to endure twenty years of the most virulent public abuse in English

---

[8] Jonathan Swift, *Works* (Dublin, 1735), i.[i]. For Faulkner's edition as a whole, see Williams, *The Text of 'Gulliver's Travels'*, pp. 31–61.

[9] 'The Political Significance of *Gulliver's Travels*', *Essays Historical and Literary* (Oxford, 1938), p. 210.

history'.[10] In the last years of Queen Anne, Swift himself had complained of the impunity with which any petty scribbler was allowed to abuse the government (*P.W.* iii. 99–100). The evidence assembled by Laurence Hanson shows that governments (Tory as well as Whig) were more willing than able to suppress printed criticism.[11] During his term of office as Secretary of State, Bolingbroke had been active in attempting to suppress anti-government libels. In October 1711 he reported to the Queen the arrest of the thirteenth author of a 'scandalous pamphlet'.[12] But none of these seems to have been successfully prosecuted. The government recognized the need to introduce legislation on the subject. In January 1712 the Queen commended it to the House of Commons. Swift was warmly in favour of such a new law: he reported it to Stella on 27 February and as early as 10 March we find him complaining that 'the Commons are very slow in bringing in their Bill to limit the Press' (*J.S.* ii. 499, 510). Nothing came of the proposal. Under George I, Bolingbroke's policies were continued and with slightly more success (this in itself shows how far the Whigs had moved from their earlier role as champions of liberty). But as earlier, printers and authors were more frequently arrested as part of a campaign of harassment than with any real hope of securing conviction.[13]

---

[10] 'The Problem of Political Allegory in *Gulliver's Travels*', *Modern Philology*, lxxiii (1976), S43.

[11] *Government and the Press 1695–1763* (London, 1936).

[12] *Letters and Correspondence*, ed. Gilbert Parke (London, 1798), i. 411.

[13] The Licensing Act, which had expired in 1695 and been allowed to lapse, was evidently too closely identified with the arbitrary, absolutist, and popish Stuarts for even Walpole to be able to attempt to revive it. Thus Matthew Tindal wrote that 'the restraint of the Press is consistent enough with Popery; but for Protestants to attempt it, is striking at the Foundation of their Religion'; *Reasons against Restraining the Press* (London, 1704), p. 8. The pamphlet was published anonymously. The association of censorship with popery and the Pretender made juries reluctant to convict, and governments reluctant to risk unsuccessful prosecutions. From a detailed study of the King's Bench indictments Donald Thomas concludes: 'Political censorship of the press between 1702 and 1730 is haphazard rather than systematic, according to the evidence of the indictments. Arrest and harassment of publishers, rather than full-scale prosecution, appears as the preferred method by which governments dealt with their critics'; 'Press Prosecutions in the Eighteenth and Nineteenth Centuries', *The Library*, 5th series, xxxii (1977), 315–32. The quotation is from p. 316. C. R. Kropf, 'Libel and Satire in the Eighteenth Century', *Eighteenth-Century Studies*, viii (1974–5), 153–68, discusses the question from a literary point of view. Kropf accepts (pp. 166–7) the

One factor which obviously inhibited the government from taking action as often as it would have liked was the fear of losing face through an unsuccessful prosecution. Thus the Whigs' impeachment of Sacheverell in 1709-10 had rebounded, making a popular martyr of Sacheverell himself and resulting in a considerable loss of popularity for the government. An action for libel against a fiction like *Gulliver's Travels* could have done the government no good. If successful, it would look like using a sledge-hammer to crack a nut; if unsuccessful, the government would look doubly foolish. Either way the book would have secured additional sales and notoriety. The safest course was to let things burn themselves out. Walpole knew that what counted in keeping him in power was the favour of the king and the votes of the House of Commons. He could safely ignore any amount of press abuse, no matter how scurrilous. The long press campaign waged by Bolingbroke in the *Craftsman* between 1726 and 1735 had little enough effect on the course of politics. Literary historians, with a professional interest in the written word, are apt to overestimate its importance and influence.

So far as is known, no part of any manuscript of *Gulliver's Travels* is extant. The earliest witness to the text is Motte's edition of 1726. We do, however, have documents that have been thought of as helping us get behind Motte's text to a reconstruction of the manuscript as it left Swift's hands. There is the very important letter of 3 January 1727 which Charles Ford wrote to Motte, complaining of errors of the press and more serious corruptions, and appending a list of corrections.[14] There is also Charles Ford's own copy of Motte's first edition with apparently authoritative corrections by Ford himself: small corrections are made in the text, but longer passages are written out on blank leaves bound in at several points in Volume II.[15] Both documents are closely

---

traditional view, which I challenge in this chapter, that Motte tampered with Swift's text to avoid prosecution.

[14] Library of the Victoria and Albert Museum, Forster MS 561. The text of the letter is printed in *Corr.* iii. 194-5; for the list of errata, see *Gulliver's Travels*, ed. Williams, Appendix I, pp. 423-31.

[15] Also in the Library of the Victoria and Albert Museum (Forster MS 8551). There are other similarly annotated copies of Motte's *Gulliver*: one, with corrections in Ford's hand, is in the Pierpont Morgan Library. Another, with corrections

associated with Charles Ford, and their importance for the
text of *Gulliver's Travels* warrants a brief account of Ford
and the kind of relationship he enjoyed with Swift.

Ford was for many years one of Swift's most intimate and
trusted friends. It seems to have been to Ford that Swift first
communicated the secret of his writing *Gulliver's Travels*.
Born in 1682, Ford was fifteen years Swift's junior. In 1705
his father died, and he lived on his estate at Woodpark,
between Dublin and Swift's living of Laracor. Many references
in the *Journal to Stella* attest the easy intimacy which Swift
and Ford enjoyed at that time. In 1712 Swift used Ford to
'copy out a small pamphlet, and send it to the press, that I
might not be known for author' (*J.S.* ii. 466). Later in 1712
Swift obtained for Ford the post of editor of the *London
Gazette*. Ford held this position until turned out by the
Whigs in September 1714, and in July and August of that
year he was the major source of political news for Swift in
retirement at Letcombe Basset. Ford's political sympathies
are evidenced by his joining Bolingbroke in France in 1715.
On his return to England he was arrested, although later
released without any charges being preferred. Between 1715
and 1718 he lived on the continent. He spent the remainder
of his life (he died in 1743) in London, with annual visits to
Dublin until 1732. Thus from personal intimacy as well as
political sympathy, Ford was well placed to receive Swift's
confidence. The frequent references to Ford in the *Journal
to Stella* most often carry the implication that Swift relaxed
and unbent with Ford. After the serious business of politics,
Swift would enjoy dinner, or a glass of wine, or an hour's
bookhunting, with his Irish companion. Ford was certainly
much in Swift's confidence about *Gulliver's Travels*, for their
letters furnish most of our evidence about its composition.[16]

---

in what Sir Harold Williams regarded as 'an unknown hand' (*P.W.* xi. 302), is in
the Armagh Public Library. David Woolley, however, regards the Armagh copy as
Swift's own: 'Swift's Copy of *Gulliver's Travels*: The Armagh *Gulliver*, Hyde's
Edition, and Swift's Earliest Corrections', *The Art of Jonathan Swift*, ed. Clive
T. Probyn (London, 1978), pp. 131-78. The complexity of the evidence and
arguments involved precludes my indicating in detail why I disagree with Woolley's
conclusions, particularly since they affect my own only indirectly.

[16] The foregoing account of Ford is based on the Introduction to the *Letters
of Jonathan Swift to Charles Ford*, ed. David Nichol Smith (Oxford, 1935).

The Ford documents can be presumed to carry almost authorial authority. But we need also to remember that Ford was capable of sharing a Swiftian joke. He would not have been Swift's chosen companion in his hours of ease in London if they had not had a sense of humour in common.

For the most part, the readings of Ford's letter to Motte and of his 'interleaved' copy have been accepted without question as Swift's: indeed, this is almost the only point of agreement between Williams and Case. Williams, it is true, thought some of them might be revisions rather than restorations, and even found them occasionally 'needless, debatable, or for the worse'.[17] But in general, scholars have accepted Ford's complaints against Motte as both substantially true and carrying Swift's authority. If the Ford readings are indeed restorations of those of the original manuscript submitted to Motte, there is no need to try to date them. But if they are, or may be, revisions, it becomes important to determine, as exactly as possible, when Swift made them. For this purpose it is necessary to discriminate between the readings in Motte's letter and those in the 'interleaved' copy.

Ford's letter to Motte is dated 3 January 1727 and was postmarked on 10 January. We can therefore confidently date its composition and the 'corrections' it contains. The most interesting feature of the letter, given that it was written in Dublin where Ford presumably had easy access to Swift, is that Ford specifically disclaims the authority of author or manuscript for the corrections he asks Motte to make: 'I bought here Capt.[n] Gulliver's Travels publish'd by you, both because I heard much Talk of it, and because of a Rumor, that a Friend of mine is suspected to be the Author. I have read this Book twice over with great Care, as well as great Pleasure, and am sorry to tell you that it abounds with many gross Errors of the Press, whereof I have sent you as many as I could find, with the Corrections of them as the plain Sense must lead, and I hope you will insert them, if you make another edition' (*Corr.* iii. 194; corrected from the MS). In the list of corrections which follows, much the larger number are trifling. In these cases (mostly only a single word is

---

[17] *The Text of 'Gulliver's Travels'*, p. 51.

involved) the 'correct' reading is given. But in a few cases, a passage is identified as corrupt without any 'correct' version being given: Motte is referred to the manuscript. By contrast, in the 'interleaved' copy (which may contain corrections of different dates) Ford confidently sets right these passages which in his letter to Motte he only (on internal evidence) identified as corrupt.

How did Motte react to Ford's letter? His scrupulous concern for the integrity of the book he had published is shown by the fact that, when (in May) he published a new edition of *Gulliver's Travels*, he adopted all of Ford's specific corrections with only the most trifling exceptions.[18] The more substantial corruptions he appears to have rejected, scoring them out on the letter.[19] It is hard to understand why Motte did this if (as Ford's letter implies) he really had an 'original' text available in which the 'correct' readings would have been found. *Gulliver* had escaped prosecution and had enjoyed a popular success. Even if Motte had prudently destroyed the original manuscript, between the receipt of the letter in January and the publication of the new edition in May, he had ample time to obtain from Ford the correct readings of the passages in question. On the other hand, if Motte had been indifferent to the correctness of the text, he could easily have ignored Ford's letter and the corrections it contained. The way Motte actually dealt with Ford's letter is best explained by supposing that, like Ford himself, he was privy to and enjoyed a typical piece of Swiftian jesting.

In later years Swift used Motte both as a publisher and as an agent in London for other purposes. When it came to the publication of the 'third' volume of the Pope–Swift *Miscellanies*, there was even a misunderstanding between Swift (who wished to use Motte) and Pope (who wanted Gilliver to get the job). On this occasion Swift wrote Motte a letter in

---

[18] Motte seems to have overlooked 'Ancestor' for 'Ancestors' (1726 ed., Part III, p. 102) and 'inferior posterior' for 'posterior' (Part IV, p. 88). He seems to have miscorrected 'whom we called Queen' to 'called a Queen' instead of to 'whom we called a Queen' (Part IV, p. 56).

[19] Some of Ford's comments are apparently underlined, others struck out. This apparent inconsistency can be explained by the supposition that the 'underlining' is really careless crossing-out. At any rate, Motte made the corrections that he did not in some way mark.

which he spoke of being 'assured of your honest and fair dealing, which I have allways found' (*Corr.* iv. 42). If Motte had really tampered with the text of *Gulliver's Travels* out of some base prudential fear of government prosecution, he would hardly have retained Swift's confidence in the way that Swift's later letters to him strongly suggest that he did. Swift's complaints about Motte's printing of *Gulliver's Travels* are probably to be taken no more seriously than his disowning to Stella of Tooke's edition of his *Miscellanies in Prose and Verse*. Motte probably did not 'correct' the longer corrupt passages because they were not in fact 'corrupt'. The supposed restorations of these passages in Ford's 'interleaved' copy are much more likely to be revisions than true corrections. Thus Williams recognized that 'the substitutions of the interleaved volume (although on this point it is impossible to speak with certainty) have the appearance of going beyond the rectification of passages omitted or altered by Motte'.[20] They are not truly restorations of what Swift wrote in 1725–6, but represent rather an intermediate stage of the text between the editions of Motte and Faulkner.

Certainty is impossible without new evidence, which is unlikely now to come to light. But reading Ford's letter in the light of Swift's love of jests and mystification makes it seem likely that the story of Motte's adulteration of the text of *Gulliver's Travels* was more of a joke than a serious complaint. If Swift, as early as January 1727, was dissatisfied with *Gulliver's Travels* it was not as a result of Motte's tampering with the text but because he now wished to rewrite parts of the book. This dissatisfaction was the natural result of some late additions, as the examples discussed below will suggest. But quite apart from any real vexation he may have felt, Swift was willing to play his usual game of disowning the publication of his work. In writing to Motte, Ford was carrying on the joke, acting the part of 'Gulliver's friend', as Swift had written to Pope, in giving out that 'that his copy was basely mangled . . . by the printer' (*Corr.* iii. 190). While Williams does speak of revisions, in general he thought that the 1735 text both 'represented Swift's last thoughts and was

---

[20] *The Text of 'Gulliver's Travels'*, p. 34.

nearer to the original manuscript from which, with excisions and alterations, Benjamin Motte printed the first edition'.[21] Swift's purposes in writing *Gulliver's Travels* changed too much over the years for this to be even possible. While we may accept Faulkner's 1735 text as representing Swift's final intentions, Motte's edition represents (in substance) a surer guide to Swift's intentions in 1726. Although Swift's stylistic changes between 1726 and 1735 are mostly for the better, his substantive alterations are often for the worse. Some of the politically significant of these changes can now be examined in the light of this conjectural reconstruction of the history of the text.

Most readers of *Gulliver's Travels* would probably be surprised to learn that the blue, red, and green threads used in Lilliput to reward dextrous politicians (I. iii. 39) were coloured, in the 1726 edition, purple, yellow, and white (*P.W.* xi. 303, 304). The minority of readers aware of the textual point would know it as an example of the way in which Swift's manuscript was censored before publication to remove politically offensive material.[22] The example is small but indicative. In 1726, the satiric point is general. The hierarchy of colours suggests silver, gold, and imperial purple in a natural progression that represents no particular system of honours.[23] Ford's letter passes over this passage, but the new colours are found in his 'interleaved' copy. The new colours are quite unmistakably those of the three major British orders: the Garter (blue), the Bath (red), and the Thistle (green).

Since there is no conceivable reason why so mild a satirical stroke should have been thought dangerous, the change is probably a revision rather than a restoration. Two of the orders, the Garter and the Bath, had recently achieved topicality or notoriety, and both in connection with Walpole. In 1725 Walpole had revived the Order of the Bath (disused since the coronation of Charles II) as an extra (and cheap)

---

[21]   Ibid., p. 2.

[22]   No one who has read the really virulent political satires of the period will make the mistake of supposing that such mild hits as these were capable of giving serious offence.

[23]   For a contemporary survey of the jungle of orders and their insignia, see John Guillim, *A Display of Heraldry*, 6th ed. (London, 1724), Part II, pp. 236-65.

source of political patronage. The new knights (one of whom was Walpole himself) were installed in June with 'the utmost Pomp, Solemnity, and Magnificance'.[24] The occasion was a demonstration (soon after the demotion of Carteret) of Walpole's political power, and it provoked satire and derision among the disaffected. An amusing example is the ballad 'Robin's Glory: or, The Procession of the Knights of the Bath'.[25] In 1726 Walpole was raised to the Garter, and again his inauguration was an occasion of much ostentation and satire. 'Sir Blue-String' became one of his accepted nicknames.[26] During his long visit to England in 1726, Swift attempted without success to convince Walpole of the wrongs of Ireland (*Corr.* iii. 131–5). The tone of this interview, so far as one can judge from the account that Swift gives in his letter to Peterborough, was cool but polite. That was in April 1726, some months before *Gulliver's Travels* was published. When Swift was next in London, in April 1727, his attitude to Walpole had become far more hostile. On 13 May he wrote to Thomas Sheridan that 'we are here in a strange Situation; a firm, settled Resolution to assault the present Administration, and break it if possible. It is certain that W — is Peevish and Discontented, stoops to the vilest Offices of hiring Scoundrels to write *Billingsgate* of the lowest and most prostitute Kind, and has none but Beasts and Blockheads for his Pen-men, whom he pays in ready Guineas very liberally' (*Corr.* iii. 207). This letter was written only about two weeks after Swift, under the pseudonym 'Richard Sympson', had been in touch with Motte about some unspecified business connected with Gulliver (*Corr.* iii. 206). It was in May 1727 that Motte published his new edition of *Gulliver's Travels*. The probability is that, motivated by an increased dislike of Walpole and the methods of his government, Swift sacrificed his originally general satiric point about the absurdity of ribbons as marks of honour (the English system would have been included, of

[24]   Boyer, *Political State*, xxix (June 1725), 524.

[25]   *Robin's Panegyrick*, Part I (London, 1729), pp. 105–6; reprinted in *Political Ballads Illustrating the Administration of Sir Robert Walpole*, ed. Milton Percival (Oxford, 1916), pp. 1–3. Swift himself may have written 'Verses on the Revival of the Order of the Bath' (1725?; *Poems* ii. 388–9).

[26]   See, for example, 'The Progress of Patriotism', *Robin's Panegyrick*, Part I, pp. 99–103.

course) in order to gratify his spleen against Walpole. But he
did not, at first, make these new colours part of the public
text of the work, although he had every chance to do so
while Motte's new edition was in preparation. For in that
edition the ribbons remain white, yellow, and purple. Swift
seems to have passed the new colours on to Ford, who entered
them in the 'interleaved' copy. Possibly they were communicated as a semi-private joke among others sympathetic to the
opposition. But in revising *Gulliver* for Faulkner's edition,
Swift made the new colours part of the public meaning of the
work. In doing so he needlessly limited his satire: it seems as
if only the British system is under attack. More seriously, the
revision has had the effect of sending the more knowing of
the book's readers on a wild-goose chase after more such
explicitly local allusions. The result has been much faulty
explication and more misreading of the book's politics. The
unknowing reader (if alerted by an editorial note) is left
either puzzled as to how much more he is missing or wonder-
ing what such topical hints are doing in a satire on the nature
of political corruption in general.

More important, however, than the ribbons (although that
passage has exercised an influence out of all proportion to its
importance) are the longer passages which Ford in his letter
to Motte identified as seriously corrupt.[27] The first of these
is Gulliver's account (III. vi. 191-2; the 1726 version is found
on p. 311) of methods of exposing plots. Ford comments
that the passage 'seems to have much of the Author's manner
of thinking, but in many places wants his Spirit'. A rewritten
version of the passage appears in his 'interleaved' copy (on
the blank pages bound in between pages 90 and 91), and this
version (with some further small changes) was printed by
Faulkner in 1735. Although the passages (in both versions)
contain several possible references to the Atterbury plot of
1722, the variants do not seem to be at all influenced by considerations of political caution.[28] Instead, they read like

[27] For an alternative approach to these passages, see Clauston Jenkins, 'The
Ford Changes and the Text of *Gulliver's Travels*', *Papers of the Bibliographical
Society of America*, lxii (1968), 1-23. Jenkins believes that the 1735 versions of
these passages are revisions, but he takes the Motte readings to be corruptions of
what Swift originally wrote (pp. 15-20).

[28] The connections between the 'plots' passages and Atterbury are skilfully

stylistic improvements.[29] Thus in 1726 the passage has a
rather flabbily meandering opening: 'should I happen to live
in a Kingdom where Plots and Conspiracies were either in
vogue from the turbulency of the meaner People, or could be
turned to the use and service of the higher Rank of them . . .'.
Ford's version begins crisply: 'in the Kingdom of *Tribnia*, by
the Natives called *Langden*, where I had long sojourned, the
Bulk of the People consisted wholly of Discoverers, Witnesses,
Informers . . .'. Unfortunately, along with the sharpness we
are given the crudely intrusive anagrams that make the satire
(as with the ribbons) needlessly specific. And while the
substance of the two passages is almost identical, the greater
directness of the 1735 version (considered in isolation) is
achieved at the cost of an increased awkwardness of context.
In 1726 Gulliver offers the account specifically as a 'project',
a means of turning to advantage the humour of a plot-happy
country. This is the source of the awkward series of condi-
tional verbs that give the impression of the passage having
been toned down: 'should I happen . . . could be turned . . . I
first would . . . when I had got . . . I would . . .'. A possible
explanation is that the passage was a late addition in 1726,
hence the original awkwardness. When Swift later revised it,
he improved the style but not the way it is fitted into its context. There is evidence that Swift tinkered with the passage a
good deal between 1727 and 1735 in the variants that are

---

and tactfully marshalled in Edward Rosenheim, Jr., 'Swift and the Atterbury
Case', *The Augustan Milieu*, ed. Henry Knight Miller and others (Oxford, 1970),
pp. 174–204. I am not persuaded, however, that the code-word 'the Gout' signify-
ing 'a High Priest' (III. vi. 191) need refer to Atterbury. In all the other examples,
the referents are things Swift disliked and they are referred to by reductive
characteristics or comparisons. Swift thought 'a standing Army' really was 'the
Plague'. The gouty high priest suggests to me a joke at the expense of the better-
fed of Walpole's compliant bench of bishops. Swift must have intended the passage
to remain intelligible after the details of the Atterbury plot had been forgotten;
he could have borrowed (or just remembered) some key words from it without
intending them to refer back to it.

[29] Herbert Davis, 'The Conciseness of Swift', *Essays on the Eighteenth Century
Presented to David Nichol Smith* (Oxford, 1945), pp. 15–32, discusses the passages
from this point of view. He regards the Motte versions as 'samples of writing which
Swift himself felt should be recognizable as something he could never have done'
(p. 28). Davis seems to allow insufficiently for the possibility that Swift might
(as I suggest) be guilty of a rough first draft, or that he might make the character
of Gulliver intentionally diffuse.

found in the various 'interleaved' copies that contain the revised version (*P.W.* xi. 311–12). But there is no sign that Motte's caution was responsible for toning down an originally more politically abrasive passage.

A second instance is Gulliver's attack on the law, illustrated by the example of the cow (IV. v. 248–50; the 1726 version is on pp. 315–17). Ford writes that this passage is:

manifestly most barbarously corrupted, full of Flatnesses, Cant Words, and Softenings unworthy the Dignity, Spirit, Candour and Frankness of the Author. By that admirable Instance of the Cow it is plain the Satyr is design'd against the Profession in general, and not only against Attorneys, or, as they are there smartly styl'd, Pettifoggers. You ought in Justice to restore those twelve Pages to the true Reading.

Again, in Ford's 'interleaved' copy a rewritten version appears (bound in between pages 68 and 69). This version is shortened and considerably improved in style. But there is nothing in the preferred version that could have given greater offence than what Motte actually printed. The natural conclusion suggested by a comparison of the two versions is that Motte printed what he received and that the Ford version is a revision. As with the 'plots' passage from Part III, the satire on the law may be a late addition which Swift had not time before publication to polish to his final satisfaction.

The one 'corruption' that Ford thought important enough to single out in the text of his letter as well as in the appended list of corrections is the paragraph describing Queen Anne's benevolent rule without a chief minister (*P.W.* xi. 318; the passage is from IV. vi, but disappeared from the 1735 text). In his letter Ford wrote that the 'Paragraph relating to her looks so very much beside the Purpose that I cannot think it to have been written by the same Author . . . it is plainly false in Fact . . . Neither do I find the Author to be any where given to Flattery, or indeed very favourable to any Prince or Minister whatsoever' (*Corr.* iii. 195). Since the passage is unfamiliar, being omitted from most modern editions and reprints that are based on Faulkner's text, it will bear quotation at length:

our She Governor or Queen having no Ambition to gratify, no Inclination to satisfy of extending her Power to the Injury of her Neighbours, or the Prejudice of her own Subjects, was therefore so far from needing a corrupt Ministry to carry on or cover any sinister Designs, that She not only directs her own Actions to the Good of her People, conducts them by the Direction, and restrains them within the Limitation of the Laws of her own Country; but submits the Behaviour and Acts of those She intrusts with the Administration of Her Affairs to the Examination of Her great Council, and subjects them to the Penalties of the Law; and therefore never puts any such Confidence in any of her Subjects as to entrust them with the whole and entire Administration of her Affairs.   (*P.W.* xi. 318.)

This passage has manifestly nothing to do with the real Queen Anne, who here serves as a peg on which to hang a very thinly veiled attack on George I and his policies. One easily recognizes most of the standard opposition charges. The 'Ambition to gratify' refers to George's desire to add Bremen and Verden to Hanover, to the 'Injury' of other states in the area and to the 'Prejudice' of the British who had to pay for the Baltic fleets that helped George acquire them. The 'corrupt Ministry' had repealed parts of the Act of Settlement on George's behalf, and carried on such 'sinister Designs' as the Bubble of 1720. The 'whole and entire Administration' in 1726 was in the hands of Walpole. The point about the 'great Council' and the 'Penalties of the Law' refers to the way the government appeared to be getting less and less accountable to parliament. Walpole's screening of the guilty ministers involved in the Bubble scandal was notorious. More generally, an unofficial cabinet was replacing the official Privy Council. Walpole actively discouraged parliamentary enquiries of any kind; this confirmed, as his role in the Bubble had earned him, the nickname of 'Screen-master general'.[30]

At first sight, the removal of the passage from Faulkner's edition in 1735 seems to run counter to the trend in revision towards greater particularity, since in this case it is Motte's text that is the more specific. But the apparent exception is actually the strongest argument against Motte having tampered with the text at all. For this is a case where Motte's reading is the more outspokenly anti-government. It must therefore be Swift's. Motte would hardly have interfered with the text to make it *more* offensive to the ministry. The most likely

[30] J. H. Plumb, *Sir Robert Walpole: The Making of a Statesman* (London, 1956), pp. 329–58.

explanation is that the 'She Governor or Queen' passage was another late addition. Like the passages already discussed, it is both rather clumsily written and rather awkwardly tied in place. It is characterized by the same rambling sentences that we find in the early versions of the 'plots' and 'cow' passages. In this case, however, Swift himself realized that the passage could not be improved by mere rewriting. Attacking George through heaping undeserved praise on Anne could only muddy the satire. He therefore decided to omit the passage altogether. In doing so, he provided us with strongly presumptive evidence that Motte did not in fact tamper with the passages identified by Ford as corrupt.[31]

To these three instances of Ford's supposed 'corruptions' it is instructive to add the incident of the rebellion of Lindalino (*P.W.* xi. 309–10). This passage was printed neither in Motte's edition nor in Faulkner's, nor indeed at all in Swift's lifetime. It is found in Ford's 'interleaved' copy (bound in between pages 70 and 71 of Part IV), from which it was first printed in 1896.[32] Its appearance in the 'interleaved' copy certainly suggests that at one time Swift intended to include the episode in texts of *Gulliver's Travels*. But its non-appearance in 1735 counts heavily against it. Most modern editions, supported by Williams, print it in the text. But I believe that Swift was right to reject the episode, and Davis right to relegate it to the textual notes. It is really a rejected idea of Swift's that happens to have been preserved through the accident of having been communicated to Ford. Its narrative mode is quite unsuited to *Gulliver's Travels*. Whatever its precise meaning, it invites detailed allegorical interpreation in a way that most of *Gulliver's Travels* does not.[33] What do the 'four large Towers' and the 'strong pointed Rock' represent, we can hardly help asking. The effect of printing the episode in the text of *Gulliver's Travels* has been to encourage readers

---

[31] Jenkins, 'The Ford Changes', cites a similar (though smaller-scale) instance. He notes that 'if Motte was afraid of prosecution, he certainly would not have substituted "Governments" for "the whole Race of Mankind" ' (p. 14). The passage in question is at II. vi. 138; original reading, *P.W.* xi. 307.

[32] In an Appendix to *Gulliver's Travels*, ed. G. A. Aitken (London, 1896), p. 399.

[33] For the interpretation of this episode, see below, pp. 101–2.

to look elsewhere for the same kind of allegory, with appalling results.

An example of the way this has happened is the story of Flimnap's lucky accident (I. iii. 39). There Gulliver describes how dangerous the rope-dancing game is to the ministers, for in demonstrating their dexterity they sometimes fall. The point Swift is making is that politicians tend to overreach themselves by being too subtle; it is part of his dislike of 'mystery' in politics. Flimnap is cited as an example: 'a Year or two before my Arrival, *Flimnap* would have infallibly broke his Neck, if one of the *King's Cushions*, that accident-ally lay on the Ground, had not weakened the Force of his Fall' (I. iii. 39). Sir Walter Scott interpreted the incident as apparently alluding 'to Walpole's dismissal from office in 1717, through the successful intrigues of Sunderland and Stanhope. The cushion which broke his fall was perhaps his interest with the Duchess of Kendal, the favourite mistress of George I'.[34] Scott's idea was hardly more than a shot in the dark, and it is surprising to find it so often repeated. But it will not stand up to scrutiny. In 1717, when Walpole left office, the Duchess (then of Munster) was one of his enemies. On 30 July 1716 he wrote to Stephen Pointz that 'the Dutchesse of Munster entered into the dispute with a more than ordinary zeal and resentment against us'.[35] Before his return to power in 1720 Walpole had conciliated the duchess; but what chiefly returned him to office was his ability to persuade the Commons to pay the debts of the king's Civil List.[36] Other factors were involved too, but the duchess was not prominent. A later incident in Walpole's career fits much better. On the accession of George II in 1727, Queen Caroline (whose ample bosom would be aptly suggested in the image of the cushion) was instrumental in Walpole's retaining power. But this was in the future when Swift wrote. More than any particular incident, Swift intended Flimnap's near-fall to illustrate one of Sir William Temple's favourite historical

---

[34] Swift's *Works*, ed. Scott (Edinburgh, 1814), xii, 51. Scott himself, of course, could not have been influenced by the Lindalino episode, which was unpublished in his lifetime.

[35] Plumb, *Sir Robert Walpole: The Making of a Statesman*, p. 227.

[36] For the circumstances of Walpole's return to power, see Plumb, pp. 285–92.

maxims, the idea of trifling circumstances affecting great historical events.[37] Any attempt to pin down this or other incidents in *Gulliver's Travels* in too topical a manner should be resisted. Walpole was only an example; it was the idea that he represented that Swift was satirizing.

The weight of the textual evidence, and what else we know about the process of composition, is that Swift conceived *Gulliver's Travels* first of all as a general satirical commentary on the follies of civilized man. In this original plan, particular examples would appear only as if by accident.[38] But towards the end of the period of composition, and after publication, Swift partially lost sight of this original aim. Yet, apart from a few details (and they do not bulk very large in the *Travels* as a whole), Swift retained a strong enough sense of his original purpose to protest against the charge of parochialism made by the Abbé Desfontaines. 'Les memes follies', he wrote, 'regnent par tout, du moins, dans tous les pays civilises de l'Europe, et l'auteur qui n'ecrit que pour une ville, une province, un Royaume, ou meme un siecle, merite si peu d'être traduit qu'il ne merite par d'etre lû' (*Corr.* iii. 226). Swift had tried to give *Gulliver's Travels* a European rather than a merely English relevance. In his political pamphlets he had referred to general principles, but there they had been used to reinforce partisan arguments. In *Gulliver's Travels* Swift could not quite resist the temptation to score a few partisan points, but they were subordinated to the expression of the general political philosophy that he had never before given himself the opportunity to expound at length. Fortunately he chose not to write a treatise but to embody it (along with much else) in a fiction that would take its place in a European tradition. Because the 1726 version is closer to this original (and in my view, at least) superior conception, readers of *Gulliver's Travels* should be given wider opportunities to read the book in this original form. Although there is no reason to exclude from the text Swift's stylistic improvements, afterthoughts such as the Lindalino rebellion and the blue, red, and green threads should be recorded either in notes or in an

---

[37] See, for example, *Miscellanea* (London, 1680), pp. 195-7; and above, pp. 27, 30. Nor should one forget the simple comic value of the incident.
[38] See below, pp. 111, 114, 118.

appendix. With these safely out of the way, readers will be much less likely to be misled into allegorizing and misinterpretation.

CHAPTER 4

Allegories and Allusions

Swift's primary purpose in *Gulliver's Travels*, like Plato's in the *Republic*, was to record in an imaginative creation for the benefit of posterity a vision of political wisdom he had been denied the opportunity of using in the service of his own time and country. This purpose was the original impulse and remained the main driving force behind the writing of *Gulliver's Travels*. But this noble aim was not inconsistent with others less exalted. Swift also wanted to expose the nonsense and follies of contemporary politicians and to put forward some moderate ideas for practical reforms. He was remarkably successful in pursuing these different aims without getting at cross purposes with himself. But he was unable entirely to avoid inviting misreading of his text. His renewed interest in English politics caused him to make *Gulliver's Travels* a little more topical that he had originally intended, and this process continued after publication. As a result, much scholarly ingenuity has been devoted to a wild-goose chase after interpretations of *Gulliver*'s politics that are more particular, topical, and personal than the nature of the satire warrants. The blue, red, and green ribbons are much to blame in this respect.

Swift's political commentaries in *Gulliver's Travels* are expressed through fables and paradigms rather than specific allegories and allusions referring to particular events and politicians. Contemporary politics should be thought of as illustrating Swift's points rather than explaining them. His purpose was to attack political corruption, not just its particular contemporary embodiment in the Walpole administration. Correspondingly, his treatment of kingship was to exemplify its ideal (in the King of Brobdingnag) and to contrast that ideal with antitypes (the Emperor of Lilliput and the King of Laputa). The fact that some of the faults of those unlikeable monarchs were also characteristics of George I does not make him in any sense their 'original'. Swift's satire could be applied to the contemporary scene, and he intended it to be; but it has no particular meanings limited to or determined by that scene.

In the *Phaedo* Socrates tells how we derive the idea of equality from seeing 'equal sticks or stones or other equal objects' (74b–c). So Swift derived the ideas of his political ideals and types from particular kings, ministers, and statesmen. But Socrates then argues that these 'equal sticks and other things' are not 'equal in the sense of absolute equality' but 'fall short of it in so far as they only approximate to equality' (74d). Similarly any actual prime minister must fall short of being like the 'ideal' prime minister that Gulliver describes to his Houyhnhnm master (IV. vi. 255), although actual prime ministers may partake of its nature and remind us of it in several respects.

The 'particular' interpretations of the political satire of *Gulliver's Travels* have a history almost as long as the book itself. Some of its earliest readers were convinced that it contained covert but ascertainable references to contemporary political events and personalities. Not much contemporary comment of this kind has been preserved, unfortunately, outside hack journalism. Soon after publication of *Gulliver's Travels* Gay reported to Swift that:

the Politicians to a man agree, that it is free from particular reflections, but that the Satire on general societies of men is too severe. Not but we now and then meet with people of greater perspicuity, who are in search for particular applications in every leaf; and it is highly probable we shall have keys published to give light into Gulliver's design. (*Corr*. iii. 182–3.)

Gay's jest was another's earnest, and the keys duly appeared. Yet it is a pity that we do not have more detailed reports than Gay's on what the 'people of greater perspicuity' in the political world thought about what Swift was trying to do.

The most extensive contemporary critique, Abel Boyer's in the *Political State of Great Britain*, is disappointingly padded with extensive quotation.[1] The same is true of the most

[1] It appeared in the *Political State* in three parts, from November 1726 to January 1727. Some of Boyer's comments are interesting, such as his identification of the Flying Island with the royal prerogative; *Political State*, xxxiii (January 1727), 27. There is a useful discussion of Boyer's criticism and techniques in Phyllis J. Guskin, ' "A very remarkable Book": Abel Boyer's View of *Gulliver's*

interesting of the separately published commentaries, Edmund Curll's *A Key, Being Observations and Explanatory Notes, upon the Travels of Lemuel Gulliver*.[2] Curll was never one to supply his readers with original matter where reprinted or pirated would suffice, and the *Key* is no exception. The greater part of its slim bulk comprises extensive quotation from *Gulliver's Travels* itself. Yet when Curll does slip in an original comment it is often valuable as an indication of an interpretation that at least occurred to a contemporary reader. Curll's technique is to guess at the likely 'meaning' of any isolated incident or allusion that occurs to him as having one. He does not, even in Part I, attempt to work out a consistent allegorical interpretation. Some of Curll's guesses coincide with modern orthodoxy, others do not. Thus he is at one with modern critics in connecting Flimnap with Walpole (p. 13), and the coloured ribbons with the major British Orders (p. 16). Sometimes he sides with one of the camps of opposing moderns, as when he identifies Reldresal with Townshend (p. 13). Elsewhere his suggestions have fallen on stonier ground, as when he identifies the Emperor of Lilliput with William III on the basis of their similar noses (pp. 8–9), when he identifies Blefuscu with Scotland (p. 20), and when he relates Gulliver's putting out the fire in the Empress's apartments with the celebrated fire at the Duc d'Aumont's (p. 21).[3] If it were not that the *Key* is an obviously hasty and opportunistic publication, and that care and integrity are the last things one looks for in a Curll production, it would be tempting to use the *Key* as evidence that contemporaries were more confused than anything else about the particular interpretation of *Gulliver's Travels*. As it is, Curll provides negative evidence that the elaborate allegory of modern

---

Travels', *Studies in Philology*, lxxii (1975), 439–53. The best general discussion of *Gulliver*'s contemporary reception is in Bertrand A. Goldgar, *Walpole and the Wits* (Lincoln, Neb., 1976), pp. 49–63.

[2] The *Key* was published under the pseudonym 'Signor Corolini' and was also issued in four separate parts. It was advertised in the *Monthly Catalogue*, no. 43 (November 1726), p. 26. Each of the *Key*'s four parts is paginated separately; the references in the text are to the first part.

[3] W. A. Speck, however, in his *Swift* (London, 1969), p. 112, sees certain features of William III in the Emperor. For the fire at the Duc d'Aumont's, see the *Journal to Stella*, 25 January 1713 (*J.S.* ii. 608).

creation was not obvious to the first audience.

Modern scholars have generally been among those 'people of greater perspicuity' of whom Gay spoke. Yet there has been no unanimity of interpretation, no building on agreed bases, and the nature and meaning of the personal political satire eludes consensus and continues to provoke debate. This itself should act as a warning, for when Swift and his contemporaries attacked a person they made sure their readers knew what they were about.

The school of 'greater perspicuity' began in earnest with Sir Charles Firth's British Academy lecture of 1919, which for the first time proposed a detailed (if not always consistent) allegorical reading of Part I and sections of Part III of the *Travels*.[4] Firth's actual interpretations prove to have worn less well than his basic idea of looking for hidden allegorical significance.[5] Firth has exercised a considerable influence on the way we read *Gulliver's Travels*, not just among the scholars who read books on the subject, but among the much larger numbers of readers who use modern annotated editions. Every such edition incorporates the results of one variant or another of the Firth hypothesis, often without recording the fact that such interpretations are hypothetical. Thus Firth's *kind* of interpretation has hardened into an orthodoxy. An occasional sceptical voice has been raised. Phillip Harth, in an article all the more trenchant for its brevity, has pointed out some of the large implausibilities and misconceptions on which the traditional readings are based.[6] The question is an important one. Swift set out to make *Gulliver's Travels* of more than local or temporary interest. If he was at all successful in this, he cannot have intended

[4] 'The Political Significance of *Gulliver's Travels*', reprinted in his *Essays Historical and Literary* (Oxford, 1938), pp. 210–41, to which subsequent references are given.

[5] The most important later refinements and variants on Firth's approach are by Arthur E. Case, 'Personal and Political Satire in *Gulliver's Travels*', in his *Four Essays on 'Gulliver's Travels'* (Princeton, 1945), pp. 69–96; Irvin Ehrenpreis, *The Personality of Jonathan Swift* (London, 1958), pp. 83–116; and Speck, *Swift*, pp. 105–20.

[6] 'The Problem of Political Allegory in *Gulliver's Travels*', *Modern Philology*, lxxiii.4 (May 1976), pt. 2, S40–7. Scepticism is also voiced by J. A. Downie, 'Political Characterization in *Gulliver's Travels*', *Yearbook of English Studies*, vii (1977), 108–20.

the particular satire on specific individuals and events that Firth and others have detected to have the kind of significance they claim for it.

This kind of misinterpretation rests on two basic misunderstandings, of the why and the how of Swift's and his contemporaries' use of satiric indirection. There is no doubt that indirection was a favourite mode among political commentators in Swift's day. A passage from Swift's *The Importance of the Guardian Considered* (1713) is often quoted to explain why:

You must know, Sir, that we have several Ways here of abusing one another, without incurring the Danger of the Law. First, we are careful never to print a Man's Name out at length; but as I do that of Mr. *St*——: So that although every Body alive knows whom I mean, the Plaintiff can have no Redress in any Court of Justice. Secondly, by putting Cases; Thirdly, by Insinuations; Fourthly, by celebrating the Actions of others, who acted directly contrary to the Persons we would reflect on; Fifthly, by Nicknames, either commonly known or stamp'd for the purpose, which every Body can tell how to apply. (*P.W.* viii. 14–15.)[7]

Swift's wit has been the cause of much misconception. The idea that such methods would evade prosecution was commonly held at the time, as it still is, but does not reflect the real legal situation.[8] Indirect 'innuendoes' were certaintly actionable. It was no legal protection to write of the 'E—— of O——d' where one meant the Earl of Oxford. Nevertheless, contemporaries seem to have been fond of the air of mystery created by such subterfuges.

The real reason for the use of indirect methods in political satire seems indeed to have been rhetorical and aesthetic rather than legal. Ridicule, in particular, was more effectively expressed through satiric fiction than through direct discourse. Nor should one discount the importance of the pleasure that readers took in the sense of belonging to a well-informed minority possessing the inside information necessary to unravel the real meaning of the latest satirical pamphlet. James

[7] I have restored the reading '*St*——' from the first edition; Davis spoils the joke by printing 'Steele' throughout.

[8] See, for example, the precedents cited in *State Law: or, The Doctrine of Libels Discussed and Examined* (2nd ed., London, [1728]), and Sgt. Parker's speech at the trial of Sacheverell, printed in *State Trials* (2nd ed., London, 1730), v. 710.

Ralph catches the spirit and the absurdity of this passion to be 'in the know' when he imagines that:

some Politicians, Informers, Reformers, and small Wits, may be very inquisitive about my half Blanks, whole Blanks, or mutilated Sentences . . . I am sensible most People love to meet with such Gaps, in order to fill them up. If every Thing was set down plain . . . it would be thought only proper for the perusal of a School boy . . . as no Author can pretend, in Writing, to please the various Humours and Desires of Mankind; let him but leave some Parts of his Work imperfect, and every Man, in finding out the Meaning, will undoubtedly strive to please himself.[9]

Ralph carries on the joke with such absurd pretended concealments in his text as 'the Dir——ors of the OPERA' (p. 21).

The same taste that enjoyed filling in the blanks, equally enjoyed working out less obvious allegories and more deeply buried allusions. But commentators who apply the allegorical method to the interpretation of *Gulliver's Travels* seem not sufficiently to have considered the ground rules that were generally observed in Swift's day. In 1715 John Hughes defined an allegory as 'a Fable or Story, in which, under imaginary Persons or Things, is shadow'd some real Action or instructive Moral; or, as I think it is somewhere very shortly defin'd by *Plutarch*, it is that *in which one thing is related, and another thing is understood*'.[10] *Gulliver's Travels* is obviously an allegory in the very broad sense that it is not really about the imaginary societies which Gulliver purports to have visited. It is in this sense that Boyer referred to them as 'ALLEGORICAL TRAVELS'.[11] But it is obviously not an allegory in the more restricted sense of a work wholly and explicitly allegorical, which is what Hughes had in mind. For he proceeds to illustrate his definition with the example of a Rubens painting in which is 'figur'd the Government of *France*, on *Lewis* the Thirteenth's arriving at Age, by a Galley. The King stands at the Helm; Mary of *Medicis*, the Queen Mother and Regent, puts the Rudder in his Hand;

---

[9] *The Touchstone* (London, 1728), pp. xxiii–iv; published anonymously. I owe this reference to Dr Vincent Carretta.

[10] 'An Essay on Allegorical Poetry', prefixed to his edition of Spenser's *Works* (London, 1715), i. xxv–lvii. The quotation is from p. xxix.

[11] *Political State*, xxxii (December 1726), 515.

Justice, Fortitude, Religion, and Publick Faith are seated at
the Oars; and other Vertues have their proper Employments
in managing the Sails and Tackle'.[12] In the case of a work of
this kind, whether a painting or a work of narrative fiction,
the spectator or reader is obviously expected and entitled to
ask, of any significant element, what it stands for. The allegory
must be clear, and consistently worked out. There must be
some means whereby we can correctly identify Justice and
not confuse it with Fortitude. Having chosen the image of the
ship of state, Rubens must maintain it; we would be offended
if Louis's mother gave him reins rather than the rudder.

No one has ever maintained that the whole of *Gulliver's
Travels* is susceptible of an allegorical interpretation of this
kind. But the idea that it contains smaller-scale examples of
such allegory is very widely assumed. The most important
example is the suggestion, first roughed out by Firth, and
since all but universally accepted, that Gulliver's adventures
in Part I are a political allegory in which Swift's real purpose
was to give a covert account of certain events in the reigns
of Anne and George I. Other allegories have been discovered
elsewhere in the book, principally in Part III. Allegorical
interpretations have been proposed for the account of the
rebellion of Lindalino (III. iii), the story of Munodi's mill
(III. iv), and the immortal Struldbruggs (III. x).[13]

If *Gulliver's Travels* were a work like the *Pilgrim's Progress*,
or like *Absalom and Achitophel*, there might arise marginal
difficulties of interpretation but we would at least feel that
we were on a track marked out by the author and that in
assuming an allegorical significance for each character and
episode we were not doing violence to the author's intentions.[14] But *Gulliver's Travels* is clearly not wholly allegorical,
and Swift has not marked out in any obvious way any parts
of the book which he wanted us to read allegorically. He
might easily have done this, for example, by using names
with suggestive etymologies where allegorical meanings were

---

[12] 'An Essay on Allegorical Poetry', pp. xxx–xxxi.
[13] Some interpretations of the Yahoos and the Houyhnhnms in Part IV are
also allegorical, but I have left them out of account as they are not political in
the same way as the examples from Part III.
[14] Harth, 'The Problem of Political Allegory', pp. S40–1.

concealed. In the absence of any such signals as Swift might
have given us, the only tests we can apply are plausibility and
consistency. Was Swift likely to have intended such a meaning, and did he work it out with such consistency that his
readers might reasonably be supposed to understand it? For
having seen that Swift was not motivated to indirection by
any legal considerations, his only reason for employing
allegory could have been the pleasure that the allegory's aptness, once discovered and understood, would have given. He
could have had no motive to implant allegories so deeply as
to be unfathomable, or so obscurely as to be incomprehens-
ible when discovered.

Hughes sets out four requirements for a successful allegory,
and by and large they seem to have been widely accepted by
contemporary allegorists. They are that the allegory be 'lively,
and surprising'; that the relationship between vehicle and
content exhibit 'Propriety, and Aptness'; that 'the Fable be
every where consistent with it self'; and that 'the Allegory be
clear and intelligible'.[15] In an example, Hughes censures
Spenser for having, in *Prothalamium*, shifted awkwardly
between allegorical and literal representations of the two
brides: 'If this had been only a Simile, the Poet might have
dropp'd it at pleasure; but as it is an Allegory, he ought to
have made it of a piece, or have invented some probable
means of coming out of it'.[16] From what he notes to be the
paucity of contemporary allegories, Hughes singles out for
praise several of Addison's papers from the *Tatler*, the *Spectator*, and the *Guardian*.[17] These examples show the taste
and bent of the period for short, self-contained, and internally
consistent allegories whose purpose is not to conceal a meaning but to make a didactic point more pleasingly. This is the
most typical use of allegory in early eighteenth-century
literature.

Swift's practice in those of his writings that are unquestion-
ably allegorical in intent conforms to the requirements of
Hughes and the example of Rubens and Addison. The sections
of *A Tale of a Tub* that are concerned with Peter, Martin, and

[15] 'An Essay on Allegorical Poetry', pp. xlvii–l.   [16] Ibid., p. xlix.
[17] For example, the 'Vision of Mirzah' in the *Spectator*, no. 159 (1 September
1711).

Jack are characterized by obvious consistency, by the use of aptly suggestive images, and by correspondence in detail between the incidents in the allegory and the historical developments they represent. Thus in Section ii, the fashions for shoulder-knots, gold lace, flame-coloured satin, silver fringe, and embroidered figures are each to be understood as referring to some episode in the gradual corruption of primitive Christianity (*P.W.* i. 49–54). The only comparable passage in *Gulliver's Travels* occurs when Gulliver tells him Houyhnhnm master of the kinds of differences of opinion that have led to war (IV. v. 246). The basic difference between the technique of *A Tale of a Tub* and the methods of *Gulliver's Travels* is well illustrated by a comparison of the religious history of Lilliput (I. iv. 49–50) with the passage from the spurious continuation of the *Tale* that gives an allegorical ecclesiastical history of England from the Reformation to about the Revolution (*P.W.* i. 286–91). The treatment of the subject in the spurious continuation of the *Tale* is characterized by exact and detailed parallels; the history of Lilliput has only a few general similarities and several features quite impossible to reconcile with historical fact. Allegorists did not play fast and loose with history in the way critics have assumed that Swift does. The episode in Lilliput is a general fable on the futility of fighting about opinions in religion; it is not an allegory of the specific events of the Reformation.

Swift's later allegories conform to the methods of *A Tale of a Tub*. 'The Story of the Injured Lady', written about 1707 although not published until 1746, is an allegorical treatment of what Swift saw as the unjust treatment of Ireland by England, especially as contrasted with the generous treatment accorded Scotland under the terms of the Union of 1707. The relationship between the three countries is figured in terms of a man and his two lovers. 'A Gentleman in the Neighbourhood had two Mistresses, another and myself; and he pretended honourable Love to us both. Our three Houses stood pretty near one another; his was parted from mine by a River, and from my Rival's by an old broken Wall' (*P.W.* ix. 3). The treatment of detail in this sentence is representative. The river stands for the Irish Sea, the wall for

Hadrian's Wall; other details are made to correspond in the same way throughout the piece. Similarly, in 'An Account of the Court and Empire of Japan', written in 1728 although not published until 1765 (*P.W.* v. 99–107), Swift offers an allegorical version of English political history from the Revolution to the accession of George II. Even apart from the obvious anagrams (Regoge, Yortes, Lelop-Aw), the reader has no difficulty in penetrating beneath the thin veil of the allegory; nor is there anything in the 'Account' that does not have some historical reference. Too much should not be made of this fact, but it is noteworthy that Swift published neither of these pieces. This may be taken as some indication of his dissatisfaction with allegory as a mode.

The same explicitness, clarity of reference, consistency, and lack of ambiguity characteristic of these Swiftian allegories are found in comparable works by his contemporaries. A few examples will illustrate how widely shared these features are. Mrs Manley's *Secret History of Queen Zarah, and the Zarazians* is a politically inspired attack on the Duchess of Marlborough.[18] It was an underground publication and so could afford to name names, but the air of mystery undoubtedly lends spice to what would otherwise be a routine piece of character assassination. The only key needed for its interpretation is a knowledge of the times and events it deals with, from the court of Charles II to the then present. Albigion is England. Zarah (Sarah) is introduced to the court of Rolando (Charles II) by her mother Jenisa (Mrs Jennings). Zarah becomes enamoured of Hippolito (John Churchill) who is currently the lover of Clelia (the Duchess of Cleveland), the king's mistress. Jenisa successfully plots to have Hippolito marry Zarah. Jarah later wins the confidence of Albania (Princess Anne), but betrays to the king her intrigue with Mulgavius (the Earl of Mulgrave). And so the story goes on, at each point an exact correspondence being kept up between the fiction and Mrs Manley's somewhat partisan version of history. There is none of the shifting about of identity or uncertainty about what events are being referred to as there is

---

[18] It was published with the false imprint 'Albigion, 1705'. For Mrs Manley's political writings, see Gwendolyn B. Needham, 'Mary de la Riviere Manley, Tory Defender', *Huntington Library Quarterly*, xii (1949), 253–88.

with the allegorical readings of *Gulliver's Travels*. Readers
with the necessary historical information have no difficulty
in identifying the various characters and incidents.

A different kind of allegory is represented by Arbuthnot's
John Bull series of pamphlets.[19] Arbuthnot transposes the
events and circumstances of the War of the Spanish Succession
into the terms of a lawsuit between John Bull (the English
people) and Lewis Baboon (Louis XIV) about who shall
enjoy the lucrative custom of Lord Strutt (the King of Spain).
No contemporary reader could have been in much doubt
about the meaning of the pamphlets. What makes *John Bull*
so enjoyable is the consistency with which Arbuthnot works
out the ramifications of his allegory, faithfully reproducing
the patterns of contemporary events in the reductive and
ludicrous terms of the parish-pump lawsuit. In two or three
cases during the course of the five pamphlets Arbuthnot does
have more than one fictional counterpart for some of the less
important characters. Thus Prince Eugene of Savoy appears
both as Hocus's clerk (i.e. Marlborough's deputy) in *Law is a
Bottomless Pit* and as Signior Benenato in *John Bull in His
Senses*, where his role is that of Esquire South's Master of
Foxhounds (i.e. envoy from the Emperor). But there is no
case where one allegorical figure represents more than one
historical person.

Closer in time to *Gulliver's Travels* is the allegorical history
of Don Ferdinando and the Bishop of Tortosa that appeared
in several numbers of the *True Briton* in 1723.[20] But the
ground rules that govern it remain basically the same as with
the earlier examples. In the first instalment (no. 15, 22 July
1723) we are given an account of the character of Don
Ferdinando (Walpole) and his enmity to the Bishop of
Tortosa (Atterbury, Bishop of Rochester). This culminates
in the accusation and trial of the bishop before the Inquisition
(the House of Lords). Important evidence is given by the Magi

[19] The five pamphlets were all published in 1712. They are collected in *The
History of John Bull*, ed. Alan W. Bower and Robert A. Erickson (Oxford, 1976).
This edition has very full annotations.
[20] The *True Briton* (collected edition, 2 vols., London, 1723) was largely the
work of the Duke of Wharton. But the allegorical papers are attributed to William
Oldisworth in Robert J. Allen, 'William Oldisworth: "the Author of the *Examiner*" ',
Philological Quarterly, xxvi (1947), 159–80.

(Walpole's decipherers of Atterbury's intercepted correspondence). The second part (no. 16, 26 July) is largely devoted to an attack on Simoni (Simon, Lord Harcourt), a former associate of the bishop who has since joined with Don Ferdinando. Harcourt, a former Jacobite and friend of Atterbury's, had made his peace with Walpole in 1721. Later episodes are concerned with Walpole's period in opposition from 1717 to 1720 (no. 20, 9 August) and with Walpole's rise to supreme power through the events of the South Sea Bubble and the deaths of Stanhope and Sunderland (no. 55, 9 December). The allegory is always clear and consistent. Don Ferdinando is always Walpole, and everything that is said about him in the allegory has some correspondence with the real Walpole. The contrast with Flimnap in *Gulliver's Travels* could hardly be more complete.

Of course, there were inconsistent and badly constructed allegories being written, but their example seems hardly relevant to the practice and interpretation of so skilful a writer as Swift. And of course, even well-informed contemporaries could make the occasional mistake in the identification of the persons meant in an allegory.[21] But such errors are typically in minor or peripheral details. The examples I have discussed are representative of competent allegorical writing of the time, and none of them present the kind of ambiguities and doubtful interpretations that are such a feature of the allegorical readings of *Gulliver's Travels*. Instead, they are characterized by explicitness, internal self-consistency, and a complete series of one-to-one correspondences between the allegory and the historical persons and events referred to. The same relationships exist between the elements of the allegory as between their historical counterparts. If *a* is *b*'s brother, he is not represented as his wife; if *x* is *y*'s father, he is not shown as his son. Nothing that is important in the historical events is left out in the allegory, nor is anything important in the allegory without some external significance. A high degree of certainty of interpretation is possible, although the odd detail

---

[21] For example, in a copy of *The Secret History of Queen Zarah* ('Albigion', 1705) now in the University of Chicago Library, the contemporary manuscript annotator wrongly identifies Clelia as Nell Gwyn (p. 7) and hesitates between the Earls of Shrewsbury and Nottingham for Salopius (pp. 62, 73).

may remain doubtful. All these requirements are fulfilled by
a work like Dryden's *Absalom and Achitophel*; none of them
are by *Gulliver's Travels*.

Even the specific parts of *Gulliver's Travels* that have been
subjected to allegorical interpretation notably fail to meet
these requirements. The best example to take first is the
story of the Lindalino rebellion in Part III.[22] This tells how
the citizens of Lindalino, the country's second city, raised a
rebellion against the King of Laputa and neutralized his usual
methods of putting down insurrections by erecting 'four large
Towers, one at every Corner of the City . . . equal in Height
to a strong pointed Rock that stands directly in the Center of
the City' (*P.W.* xi. 309). Fixing loadstones on each of these
five eminences prevents the king lowering the Flying Island
over the city, and the king is forced to redress the grievances
complained of: 'great Immunitys, the Choice of their own
Governor, and other the like Exorbitances'. Case regarded
this episode as 'an allegorical account of the Irish resistance,
in 1722–24, against the introduction into the country of
copper coins manufactured by an English ironmonger named
Wood'.[23] The story of the struggle against Wood's halfpence,
and the key role played by Swift's *Drapier's Letters* in the
opposition to the project, are well known.[24] Since the
episode occurred just at the time when Swift was writing
Gulliver's Travels, one might well have expected Swift to
incorporate some reference to his recent triumph into his
new book.[25] But if we reread the Lindalino episode with an
open mind, the fact is that it contains nothing and no one
that can stand for either the Drapier, Wood, the halfpence, or
the Duchess of Kendal through whom he obtained the patent.
Case is actually rather hard pressed to find any details in the
episode susceptible of relevant allegorical interpretation. In
virtual desperation he suggests that the 'four large Towers'

[22] For the textual questions raised by this episode, see above, pp. 85–6.

[23] *Gulliver's Tavels*, ed. Arthur E. Case (New York, 1938), p. 180; see also
Case, *Four Essays*, pp. 82–4.

[24] The fullest treatment is in *The Drapier's Letters*, ed. Herbert Davis (Oxford,
1935).

[25] Although his sense of the exceptional conditions prevailing in Ireland would
have made him reluctant to give it much attention in a work designed for the
whole of Europe; see 'Maxims Controlled in Ireland' (*P.W.* xii. 129–37).

are 'perhaps the Grand Jury, the Irish Privy Council, and the two Houses of the Irish Parliament'. The eight months delay in the king's hearing of the rebellion is explained as an 'implication . . . that George's ministers did not always keep him informed about state affairs'.[26] All this would have surprised Swift and his readers. When his contemporaries represented four things so different as a grand jury, a Privy Council, and two Houses of Parliament, they did not represent them identically as Case's interpretation does. The eight month's delay would correspond to some significant lapse of time, not to some unconnected question. And they would certainly have included in the allegory figures representing Wood and the other major factors and people.

It has been necessary to dwell thus long on these patent absurdities because they are so regularly taken solemnly and seriously, and commentators and annotators seem never to pause to ask themselves whether their basic premisses are plausible or not. In a true allegory, one which Swift might have expected his readers to understand, the details given would all mean something, and every important element would have its allegorical representation. In fact, the episode is a general fable of successful resistance to tyranny. Its moral is that force cannot keep a brave and united people enslaved. Its lesson was certainly applicable to Ireland. But so it was to contemporary England, which Swift saw as groaning under the yoke of a tyrannical king abetted by a corrupt Whig government. And so it was to France, the remoteness of whose court from its people would have been aptly symbolized by the Flying Island.

After Gulliver has left Laputa and is staying with the unfashionably conservative Lord Munodi, he hears the story of Munodi's mill: how he was forced by the projectors to build a less convenient mill than the one he already owned, and how the project's expensive failure was blamed on Munodi himself (III. iv. 177–8). Case explains the old mill as 'the old English system of providing revenue from taxes sufficient to defray current expenses without incurring a national debt'. The new mill is 'the South Sea Company, a highly speculative

<hr/>

[26] *Gulliver's Travels*, ed. Case, p. 181.

venture' that ended in disaster.[27] Here, as with the Lindalino episode, there are insuperable objections to Case's interpretation. The details of the South Sea scheme cannot conceivably be made to fit the story of Munodi's mill. Oxford was at the height of his power when the scheme was floated, not 'not very well with the Court' as Munodi was (III. iv. 178). Case blames Defoe for the scheme, but in the *Examiner* Swift regards it as an example of Oxford's transcendent financial genius (*P.W.* iii. 170). And so on.

If we feel a need to allegorize the episode, there is much less difficulty involved in reading it as an allegory of Bolingbroke's relations with the Pretender. For Bolingbroke, like Oxford, has been identified as the original of Munodi.[28] Bolingbroke fled to France in 1715 when he was indubitably 'not very well at Court' and embarked on a highly speculative career as the Pretender's Secretary of State. The failure of the 1715 rising was blamed on him, although it was certainly not his fault more than another's. At the time of writing, Bolingbroke was still out of favour and living in retirement as Munodi was. The design of the new mill replacing the old is a better type of an attempt to replace one dynasty with another than it is of a trading and financial concern. I am not, of course, proposing this as a serious interpretation of the incident, but merely as an example to show how easily such allegories are generated by a little history and a little more critical ingenuity. As with the Lindalino rebellion, the true interpretation is a general one. The mill is an emblem not of financial orthodoxy but of paternalism, symbolizing harmonious relations between landlord and tenants. Thus Munodi's estate typifies Swift's nostalgic ideal of rural old England. If the episode of the mill is more than an example of projecting madness, it suggests the increasing tendency of men of landed estates to speculate in the funds and with projects. This is a more sensible way to link it with the Bubble of 1720 than through Oxford's old connection with the project, if any particular link is needed. The disaster of the Bubble was not connected with Oxford's original scheme

---

[27] *Gulliver's Travels*, ed. Case, pp. 189, 190; see also Case, *Four Essays*, pp. 88–9.

[28] See below, pp. 118–21.

(which was sound enough) but was the result of the company's later, more ambitious, scheme to take over the whole of the unfunded national debt. It was a typical Whig job (the Duchess of Kendal and the chief ministers were well bribed) of the kind that Swift believed to be at the root of England's moral decline.

It may seem superfluous to argue at such length against Case's kind of allegorical reading. But such readings are still being proposed. The following example may seem so fantastic that refutation would be superfluous, but it appeared in a highly respected journal and its argument is elaborately and learnedly documented.[29] Various interpretations of the meaning of the immortal Struldbruggs (III. x) have been put forward, but few readers can have thought to connect them with the French Academy. The idea that Swift's warning against the unreasonable desire for length of days was directed not against a common human frailty but a specific French institution is absurdly reductive. Fortunately it is nonsense. Rather than refute the arguments in favour of the identification at tedious length, it will be sufficiently illustrative for the present discussion of Swift's supposed 'allegories' to take one representative detail and then to question the general propriety of the interpretation.

When Gulliver leaves Luggnagg, he is given a letter of introduction from the king to the Emperor of Japan. The King of Luggnagg's seal is '*A King lifting up a lame Beggar from the Earth*' (III. xi. 216). As one of a series of points supposed to connect Luggnagg with France, this seal is supposed to represent Louis XIV and his natural son, the Duc du Maine, whom Louis legitimated.[30] The Duc du Maine was hardly a beggar, but he was lame. But if the seal calls for such specific allegorical interpretation (and I do not for a moment suppose that it does), there is a much readier pair to hand. Why may it not rather represent George I promoting Benjamin

---

[29] Robert P. Fitzgerald, 'The Allegory of Luggnagg and the Struldbruggs in *Gulliver's Travels*', *Studies in Philology*, lxv (1968), 657–76. It has been taken seriously; see the review by Maurice J. Quinlan, *Philological Quarterly*, xlviii (1969), 396. Apart from the absurdity of its major contention, Fitzgerald's article does make some valuable points about Swift's knowledge of and interest in France and French life.

[30] Fitzgerald, p. 660.

Hoadly (who, in common with the Duc du Maine, was lame) to the bishoprics of Bangor, Hereford, and Salisbury? Again, I offer this suggestion only to illustrate how easily such interpretations can be generated if they are not controlled by a sense of general probability. The real import of the king's seal is that it is emblematic of the ideal exercise of kingly power, which Swift believed to be a trust from God to be exercised for the benefit of the people ruled. The incongruity between the king's action on his seal, and the etiquette of his audience chamber where '*to lick the Dust before his Footstool*' was a privilege and 'more than Matter of Form' (III. ix. 204) is complete.

Setting aside the patent absurdity of the Duc du Maine and his lameness, we may apply to the idea of the Struldbruggs representing the Academy Hughes's second rule for allegories, 'Propriety, and Aptness', in the relationship between vehicle and content. The wild disparities between Swift's race of miserable immortals and the French Academy strike one at once. The only real point of contact is the designation 'immortal'. If Swift had wanted to satirize the Academy, he had no need to hide his design and could have done so directly enough. The Academy had no spies on English soil on the lookout for scandalous innuendoes and ready to complain to the government. No purpose could be served by covert allusion. Swift could easily and effectively have satirized the Academy either through a Lilliputian institution or through the Academy of Lagado. In fact, of course, Swift had no desire to do so because he was an admirer of the Academy. There is the clearest evidence of this in the *Proposal for Correcting the English Tongue* that he addressed to Oxford in the palmy days of 1712. Swift hoped that after the peace negotiations were completed the government would have time and energy to spare for the project. Government patronage of literature and men of letters was one of his favourite schemes. It was a main purpose in the creation of 'The Society', an informal dining club that was supposed to combine politics with wit.[31] The idea that Swift characterized the original of one of his favourite projects as the repulsive Struldbruggs is grotesque and absurd.

[31] Irvin Ehrenpreis, *Swift*, ii (London, 1967), 503.

These three examples from Part III illustrate the absurdities that scholarly exegesis can fall into by neglecting the most elementary criteria for recognizing allegories in the works of Swift and his contemporaries. These are general probability, internal consistency, and lack of ambiguity. The whole point of such allegories was not to conceal but to be understood. To bury the meaning so deeply that the allegory could neither be recognized nor certainly interpreted if discovered was self-defeating. But the examples discussed so far are hardly crucial for our understanding of *Gulliver's Travels* as a whole. They affect only details. The case of the supposed political allegory of Part I is quite different, for it affects our reading of the book as a whole. Whether Gulliver is Swift, Oxford, Bolingbroke, some variable combination of the three, or just plain Gulliver, is important. For in the vain pursuit of the chimerical allegory critics and the readers they influence have been in danger of missing the moral wood through too close an attention to the supposedly allegorical trees.

The school of allegory began with Sir Charles Firth, although his interpretation is more like a system of allusions that an allegory proper. Rather than taking issue with the Firth version, however, it is more profitable to consider directly the improved and elaborated interpretation put forward by Case, since it has fewer loose ends and inconsistencies than Firth's. Case's main argument was that Gulliver's adventures in Part I represented 'the joint political fortunes of Oxford and Bolingbroke during the latter half of Queen Anne's reign'.[32] This allows Case to use points of contact between what happens to Gulliver and the careers of both men. But it would have been a most unusual proceeding even in the case of two allied politicians to have joined them in this way, and quite unthinkable in the case of two men like Oxford and Bolingbroke whose rivalry was one of the main facts about the administration and one of the major factors in its collapse. What point could be served by an allegorical representation so confused that it could not show such a basic fact? Nor is there any event during Gulliver's stay in Lilliput that can represent the Queen's change of ministry in

---

[32] Case, *Four Essays*, p. 70.

1710, an event crucial to any history of Queen Anne's reign and of paramount importance in Swift's interpretation of it. A third, and no less serious, objection is that Case's interpretation hopelessly conflates the reigns of Anne and George, making Anne (the Empress) George's wife. No contemporary allegorist could have been guilty of such an absurdity, much less Swift. Few events of the period had such a decisive effect within hours as the death of Anne on the morning of 1 August 1714. Overnight the Tory cause was in ruins. Nor does one need to know very much about Anne's attitude to George as her successor to see how ludicrous it is to suppose her represented as his wife. No Grub Street hack would have botched his job as badly as Case's reading makes Swift botch his.

An amusing illustration of the regularity expected in contemporary allegories is afforded by a pair of pamphlets written about the time that *Gulliver's Travels* was published and plausibly attributed to Henry Carey: *A Learned Dissertation on Dumpling* and *Pudding and Dumpling Burnt to Pot: or, A Compleat Key to the Dissertation on Dumpling*.[33] The *Dissertation* is a satire on political corruption. There are a few hits at particular targets, but it is certainly not an allegorical history. The *Key* pretends to ascribe the *Dissertation* to Swift, and in offering what is obviously intended as a jestingly absurd explanation of the *Dissertation*'s supposed allegorical significance, mockingly chides him for being careless and inconsistent: 'here, begging Mr. D——n's Pardon, I cannot but think his Wit has out run his Judgment; for he puts the Cart before the Horse, and begins at the latter Part of Sir **** Administration: But this might be owing to too plentiful a Dinner . . . The Author of the Dissertation, is a very bad Chronologist; for at *Page* 10. we are obliged to go back to the former Reign, where we shall find the lubberly Abbots (*i.e.*) the High Church Priests, misrepresenting Sir *John*'s Actions,

---

[33] The two pamphlets were published (anonymously) in London in February 1726 and April 1727 respectively. There is a reprint of the two together with an Introduction by Samuel L. Macey (Los Angeles, 1970; Augustan Reprint Society, no. 140); the quotations in the text are from this. Macey regards Carey as the author. The *Key* is largely a good-humoured attack on Swift, currently rumoured to be about to do a deal with the Walpole Government.

and never let the Q—— alone, till poor Sir *John* was discarded'
(pp. 18-19, 21). There are two jokes going on in these passages. One is the absurdity of the interpretations that are
being advanced, the other is the supposition that (after a
good dinner) Swift could have been a sloppy enough writer
to have meant them. The jokes would lose their point if the
interpretations were not patently absurd, or if Swift really
could have written so clumsily as the way the *Key* interprets
the *Dissertation*. Case's reading of Part I of *Gulliver's Travels*
is of the same kind as the *Key*'s of the *Dissertation*, playing
fast and loose with chronology and even personal identities.

One example of the unlimited powers of conflation and
transposition that Case assumes will suffice, the incident in
which Gulliver puts out the fire in the imperial palace by
urinating on it (I. v. 55-6). Sir Walter Scott, and, following
him, Sir Charles Firth, thought that the Empress's prudish
and ungrateful reaction to Gulliver's great service was a
reference to Queen Anne's attitude to Swift's writings: *A
Tale of a Tub* according to Scott, the licentiousness of his
political pamphlets according to Firth.[34] Case, however,
interprets Gulliver here as standing for Oxford. He cites the
letter to Swift in which Erasmus Lewis gives the ostensible
reasons for the queen's death-bed dismissal of Oxford: 'that
he never came to her at the time she appointed, that he often
came drunk, that lastly to crown all he behav'd himself
towards her with ill manner indecency & disrespect' (*Corr.* ii.
86). In Case's mind, Oxford's bibulousness and peace policy
make a happy combination: 'The brilliance of Swift's symbol-
ism is now clear. In a single action he embodied both the
political and the personal charges against Oxford. Gulliver
saved the palace, though his conduct was both illegal and
indecent: Oxford saved the state, in return for which incidental illegalities and indecencies should have been overlooked.
But prudery was stronger than gratitude.'[35] Not so brilliant,
however, for as Ehrenpreis later pointed out, it was not the
queen but George I and the Whigs who objected to the means

---

[34] Swift's *Works*, ed. Scott (Edinburgh, 1814), xii. 75 (Scott admits it is
'perhaps a strained interpretation of this incident'); Firth, *Essays*, pp. 215-16;
Case, *Four Essays*, pp. 75-6.
[35] Case, *Four Essays*, p. 76.

used to negotiate the peace.[36] And it was Bolingbroke, rather than Oxford, whose character and morals were obnoxious to the queen.

Despite his correction of Case, Ehrenpreis retains his basic reading of the incident, merely making the Empress represent Whig opinion rather than Queen Anne. This is certainly an improvement. Ehrenpreis also bolsters his argument by drawing a parallel with a pamphlet written under Swift's direction during the course of the Tory ministry. A similar image is used: 'But the Quarrelling with the Peace, because it is not exactly to our Mind, seems as if One that had put out a great Fire should be sued by the Neighbourhood for some lost Goods, or damag'd Houses; which happen'd (say they) by his making too much Haste' (*P.W.* viii. 194). Ehrenpreis even cites Renaissance writers who used the image of putting out a fire for making peace. But the dissimilarities are enormous. If the fire has an allegorical significance, it must stand for some palace intrigue; the war is already represented in the supposed allegory by the war between Lilliput and Blefuscu. Gulliver's actions could be interpreted as Swift's trying to make peace between Oxford and Bolingbroke. But there comes a time when we have to call a halt to this and similar exercises in critical ingenuity. The political events of Gulliver's stay in Lilliput are the commonplaces of contemporary history: war, peace, impeachments, trials, intrigues, ingratitude.[37] Unless a more consistent correspondence between the events in Lilliput and the events which they are supposed to represent can be demonstrated than has been the case so far, the presence of a political allegory, as distinct from isolated political allusions, must be regarded as intrinsically improbable and certainly unproven.

The ease with which interpretations of the type now current can be generated can be illustrated by my proposing a new one, not as a serious suggestion but as an example of how fatally easy they are to construct. If we assume that Gulliver is neither Swift, nor Oxford, nor Bolingbroke, but England itself, a plausible allegory of the events of the War of the Spanish Succession can be constructed. Blefuscu is

[36] *The Personality of Jonathan Swift*, pp. 87–8.
[37] Harth, 'The Problem of Political Allegory', p. S42.

France. Lilliput represents the Empire, and the Emperor the (real) Emperor. Gulliver–England is cast in the role of arbiter of Europe. At first he sides with the Emperor, to counter the threatened invasion of imperial territory by the Emperor of Blefuscu (Louis XIV). But when the Emperor's demands become unreasonable, he refuses to continue to support him. Historically this is the point (about 1709) when Whig and Tory war aims began significantly to diverge. The Tories were for preserving the balance of power by negotiating a peace rather than fighting on for the imperial advantage. Gulliver's bringing home the Blefuscan fleet represents what Swift saw as England's shouldering (a neat literal-metaphorical correspondence here) the major burden of the war effort, while getting nothing in return (Gulliver gets only his title as a reward). The fire in the palace represents the impasse in Spain, only resolved by the separate peace. Gulliver's flight represents England's siding with France against her former allies. This interpretation, even as roughed out here, involves fewer inconsistencies than the Firth–Case–Ehrenpreis version, and is consistent with Swift's views on the war as set out in *The Conduct of the Allies* and other pamphlets of the time. It is also closer to the real significance of Part I in that it avoids the personalities and the paying-off of old scores that figure too largely in current interpretations. It can hardly be over-stressed that Swift's primary purpose in *Gulliver's Travels* was not the refighting of the lost battles of the last years of Anne but the illustration of his political ideas and their application to the whole course of European history.

Part I of *Gulliver's Travels* is a political fable illustrating some of Swift's favourite themes and political maxims. For example, one of his 'Thoughts on Various Subjects' is that 'Arbitrary Power is the natural Object of Temptation to a Prince; as Wine or Women to a young Fellow' (*P.W.* iv. 244). This maxim is instanced in the Emperor of Lilliput. In historical fact, it applied more to Louis XIV than to George I. Other themes are the role of private resentments in determining public policies, the corruptions of courts, the rewards of the undeserving, and the neglect of the worthy. Such themes are apparent to every reader, and there would be no point in enumerating them if they had not become somewhat obscured

by the needless particularity of the allegorizers. The reason
one has to argue against the allegory is not merely that it is
unnecessary but that it is actually misleading. The plunge
into the depths and obscurities of allegory ends in a neglect
of the clear and obvious meanings that Swift placed conveniently on the surface of his work. Obscurity and ambiguity
were not his faults. He knew perfectly how to make his
meanings plain.

To argue against an allegorical reading is not, of course,
automatically to exclude the possibility of some more limited
'particular reflections'. If there is no allegory, there may still
be covert allusions to person and events. Here the criteria to
be applied are much less rigorous than in the case of allegories,
for allusion is a hit-and-run method of satire. Swift's contemporaries were disposed to find veiled hints and allusions
almost everywhere. The least resemblance of character or
situation was enough. This is not to say that Swift intended
such identifications to be made. In approaching the question
of personal satire in *Gulliver's Travels*, we need to make a
careful distinction between a portrait and what I would call
a paradigm. A portrait is intended to be recognized as a
representation, selective and distorted perhaps, of an individual. A good example is the character of Crassus in the *Examiner* (no. 27, 8 February 1711), which was intended and
understood to reflect solely on the Duke of Marlborough
(*P.W.* iii. 83-5). A paradigm, on the other hand, is neither
based on nor intended to suggest a particular individual. It is
a character-type which may apply to, or recall, several individuals, but none more than another. A portrait is a 'closed'
form: Crassus refers to the Duke of Marlborough, and no one
else. A paradigm is an 'open' form: it may suggest to the
reader any number of particular examples without going
beyond the author's meaning. *Gulliver's Travels* is full of such
paradigms, not portraits.

As with the question of allegory, it is worthwhile to begin
by establishing some of the rules of the game as contemporaries played it. There is an excellent example in the *Examiner*
(no. 17, 30 November 1710), where Swift constructs an
analogy between a master with a set of unruly servants and
Queen Anne with a set of rascally Whig ministers. The piece

is one of Swift's many attempts to justify the Queen's recent dismissal of her Whig ministers. 'Suppose I should complain,' Swift begins, 'that last Week my Coach was within an Inch of overturning, in a smooth, even Way, and drawn by very gentle Horses; to be sure, all my Friends would immediately lay the Fault upon *John*, because they knew, he then *Presided* in my Coach-Box' (*P.W.* iii. 25). He goes on to detail a parallel series of charges against the conduct of 'Mr. *Oldfox* my *Receiver* . . . *Charles* and *Harry*, my two *Clerks*' and '*Will Bigamy*, the *Seneschal* of my Mannor'. What is notable about this passage is the plethora of clues that Swift gives us to help identify the subjects of his satire. The Whig ex-ministers aimed at are John, Lord Somers, Lord President of the Council; the Earl of Godolphin, Lord Treasurer; Charles Spencer, Earl of Sunderland, and Henry Boyle, the two Secretaries of State; and William, Lord Cowper, Lord Chancellor. Four out of the five figures in the satire are given the same Christian names as their real-life originals, and all five have a corresponding function. Two have allusive nicknames. Godolphin had been known as 'Volpone' since at least 1704, and since 1709 it had become commonplace.[38] 'Oldfox' is an obvious pun on 'Volpone'. Cowper's nickname refers to a scandal then current about him, that he had contracted a bigamous marriage with a girl to seduce her. The currency of the story about the time Swift was writing is illustrated by the elaborate version of it that appears in the story of Hernando (Cowper) and Louisa in Mrs Manley's scandalous novel, the *Secret Memoirs . . . of Atalantis* (1709). At one point, Hernando is credited with a speech in favour of polygamy.[39] In sum, we are given eleven clues to the identities of the five figures. And this is typical, not Swift's satiric overkill. When Swift or his contemporaries wanted their personal satire to be identified, they never

---

[38] 'Volpone' stands for Godolphin in William Shippen's *Moderation Display'd* (London, 1704), p. 8. The poem was published anonymously. The sobriquet achieved notoriety when Henry Sacheverell referred to the 'crafty Insidiousness of such wiley Volpones' in his sermon *The Perils of False Brethren* (London, 1709), p. 21. See Geoffrey Holmes, *The Trial of Doctor Sacheverell* (London, 1973), p. 68; and for other examples (including the cognate 'Sir Fox'), p. 310, n. 70.

[39] *Secret Memoirs and Manners . . . from the New Atalantis* (London, 1709), i. 219–20 (published anonymously).

thought they could give too many clues. The satirist was expected to display his skill not by how obscure he could make his writing but through the aptness of his analogies and the ingenuity of their working-out. The more details that could be pressed into service, the better. Thus the satiric point of Swift's *Examiner* was to reduce the discarded Whig politicians to the level of farmyard crooks. His skill was shown in the aptness and the detailed working-out of the metaphor. Any ambiguity about who was meant would have reduced its effectiveness.

There is a passage in *Gulliver's Travels* superficially similar to the *Examiner* no. 17. Shortly after Gulliver's refusal to co-operate in the Emperor of Lilliput's plan to reduce Blefuscu to a province, a group of Lilliputian ministers intrigue against Gulliver. They are Skyresh Bolgolam, the High Admiral; Flimnap, the High Treasurer; Limtoc, the General; Lalcon, the Chamberlain; and Balmuff, the Grand Justiciary (I. vii. 67-8). Bolgolam and Flimnap have roles in other parts of the narrative, but the only appearance of the other three is in this passage. Nevertheless, Case tried to identify them all.[40] The two possible kinds of clue are their names and their functions. Attempts have been made to wring significance out of the personal names, but they do not carry conviction.[41] This leaves the functions, and on the analogy with the *Examiner* we might suppose that this would be enough. On the assumption that the conspiracy against Gulliver was an allegory of the Whig impeachment of Oxford in 1715, Case identified the Lilliputians as Nottingham, Walpole, Marlborough, Devenshire, and Cowper. It is not necessary to reject Case's premiss (as I do) to find these identifications unconvincing, for they neither fit exactly with the five functions named by Swift nor with the five most prominent of Oxford's enemies. Any attempt to decipher the conspirators against Gulliver really breaks down in view of the fact that, in England at this time,

[40] Case, *Four Essays*, p. 77. For a sceptical critique, see Downie, 'Political Characterization in *Gulliver's Travels*', pp. 112-14.

[41] For example, H. D. Kelling, 'Some Significant Names in *Gulliver's Travels*', *Studies in Philology*, xlviii (1951), 761-78; Paul Odell Clark, 'A *Gulliver* Dictionary', *Studies in Philology*, l (1953), 592-624. Clark's treatment of the subject is greatly superior to Kelling's, but for a judicious appraisal of its difficulties see Martin Price's review of Clark, *Philological Quarterly*, xxxiii (1954), 301-2.

neither the Lord Admiral nor the Lord Chamberlain was very important.[42] Swift cannot, therefore, have intended the 'clues' of the characters' functions to be used to identify them. And all we know about Limtoc is that he was the general. In military obscurity he must remain.

If Swift had wanted his readers to connect the Lilliputian politicians with their English counterparts he could easily have made their functions uniformly suggestive, as in the *Examiner* paper. His making, instead, one of the group High Admiral strongly suggests a deliberate indication that no actual group was in his mind. The Lilliputian ministerial intrigue was intended, in my view, as a paradigm of the factious combinations of self-interested and ambitious politicians. Gulliver's calling them both a 'Cabal' (I. viii. 76) and a 'Junta' (I. v. 54) would have suggested the two most important examples of such groups in recent English history: the Cabal of the reign of Charles II (Clifford, Arlington, Buckingham, Ashley, and Lauderdale) and the Junto of the reigns of William III and Anne (Halifax, Wharton, Somers, Orford, and Sunderland). Swift was certainly not intending to represent either group, but rather to create a paradigm of which both groups would have been examples. It was a helpful coincidence that both groups were five in number, exactly the kind of coincidence out of which satiric capital can be made.[43]

---

[42] Firth used as evidence in favour of Nottingham as Bolgolam the fact that he had, in the 1690s, been an Admiralty commissioner (*Essays*, pp. 217-19). The identification was also partly based on the supposition (now generally discredited) that *Gulliver's Travels* as it stands incorporates some pre-1714 material. For Bolgolam could not have been written as a character of Nottingham after 1715, when he resigned from the government in protest at what he regarded as the severe treatment of the rebels. If *Gulliver's Travels* were a Renaissance play, badly printed from a manuscript of doubtful authority, such a supposition might be tenable. On the theory that Motte softened the satire when he printed the book, the same kind of argument is sometimes used to explain loose ends of interpretation. But we know that Swift carefully revised and transcribed the *Travels*, and I have argued above (pp. 76-85) that Motte did not tamper with the text.

[43] Swift's association of the number five with ministerial combinations is illustrated by a slip he makes in one of his pamphlets. Recalling his early *Discourse of the Contests and Dissensions*, he describes it as 'upon the subject of the five great Lords' (*P.W.* viii. 119). Frank H. Ellis, in his edition of the *Discourse* (Oxford, 1967), attributes the slip to a confusion between the four lords and the five Kentish Petitioners (p. 175); but it seems more likely that Swift was confusing them with the junto.

If we turn from Gulliver's enemies to his 'friend' Reldresal (the Emperor's Secretary for Private Affairs), his character is no easier to connect with a historical figure. There was no equivalent office in England, nor do we know enough of his character to hazard an identification. Nevertheless, attempts have been made to connect him with Carteret, Stanhope, and Townshend.[44] All that these three seem to have in common is that, as Whigs of the period go, they are men of above-average ability and integrity. Reldresal is largely a functional character, needed by the mechanics of the plot. If he has any further significance, it is as a paradigm of the trimming politician, the false friend whose assistance (getting a death penalty commuted to blinding) turns out to be illusory. The same can be said of Bolgolam, who represents a type of apparently motiveless malignity common in the court life of the day.

The remaining Lilliputian politician to be considered is Flimnap the Treasurer. Few details of the allegorical interpretation of Part I are more firmly or widely accepted than the identification of Flimnap with Walpole. The idea has a long history, going back to Curll's *Key* and unquestioned since.[45] But a moment's unprejudiced reflection is enough to raise serious doubts. Flimnap is currently the royal favourite (although he once nearly fell from power). He is High Treasurer, a peer of the second rank, morose in character, and jealous of his wife. The points of contact with Walpole are the royal favour and his office as First Lord of the Treasury. In personal character he was a bluff, hearty, agreeable, and good-humoured man, indifferent to his wife's infidelities. He maintained his estranged wife on quite the same extravagant scale as he lived himself.[46] There was no reason why Swift could not have made Flimnap a character of this type. It was certainly not fear of prosecution, for in contemporary satires one usually recognizes Walpole by his

[44] Firth, *Essays*, pp. 222–3 (Carteret); *Gulliver's Travels*, ed. Harold Williams (London, 1926), p. 462 (Stanhope); Case, *Four Essays*, p. 78 (Townshend).

[45] Even the sceptical Downie regards 'the identification of Flimnap as Walpole' as beyond dispute ('Political Characterization in *Gulliver's Travels*', p. 108).

[46] J. H. Plumb, *Sir Robert Walpole* (London, 1956–60), i. 161, ii. 70.

physical characteristics. To interpret Flimnap as Walpole involves using both resemblances and differences (which are then interpreted ironically). This is extremely unsound as a methodology, for by this means almost any character can be connected with almost any historical figure. It is also circular. Only by deciding that Flimnap represents Walpole can we know which of his characteristics are to be interpreted directly and which ironically. If we look at Flimnap without any pre-conceptions, we find as much resemblance to the other 'prime ministers' of Swift's experience as to Walpole. The fact that Swift makes Flimnap a peer and Lord Treasurer suggests that he did not have Walpole particularly in mind; Godolphin and Oxford had been both, Walpole was neither. Swift intended Flimnap as a paradigm of the typical royal favourite or prime minister, not as a portrait of any particular example of the species.

Two of the characters in *Gulliver's Travels* have been iden-tified as satiric portraits of George I: the Emperor of Lilliput and the King of Laputa. Swift certainly disliked George I sufficiently to regard him as an example of the typically bad monarch.[47] But whether either of the imaginary monarchs can be regarded as specifically aimed at him is open to doubt. Some of the supposed parallels turn out to be more apparent than real. For example, his ambitions to enlarge his electorate might seem to be glanced at in the territorial ambitions of the Emperor of Lilliput. But if the Emperor suggested any par-ticular king to Swift's contemporaries, it would have been Louis XIV and his ambitions for a universal monarchy (*P.W.* i. 202). That Louis's ambitions were real to his contempor-aries, even after his fortunes took a turn for the worse, is clearly seen in (for example) Archbishop King's opinion in one of his letters to Swift (*Corr.* i. 298). The public aspect of the Emperor's display of kingship (his impressive stature, his horsemanship, his bravery, his commanding aspect) would

---

[47] See above, pp. 55–6, 58–9, 63–4, for Swift's attitude to George I. My conclusions here are shared by George's latest biographer. In *George I: Elector and King* (London, 1978), Ragnhild Hatton writes: 'Rereading *Gulliver's Travels* in search of comments on Walpole and George, the historian is forced to the conclusion that it is a general commentary on life in the states and societies of the time and that later editorial comments have provided more references to contemporary figures than are really there' (p. 259).

also more naturally have suggested Louis than George. Case argues, predictably, that here we have irony at work. But as with the case of Flimnap, one cannot reasonably count both resemblances and differences. Portraiture by opposites is fair enough; but a mixture of description and irony could only result in confusion. The one substantial point that connects the Emperor of Lilliput with George I is the issue of clemency. But George I was not the only monarch (as Swift saw it) to make hypocritical pretences at mercy at the very moments of greatest cruelty (I. vii. 72). A close parallel has been observed between what Swift says of the Emperor of Lilliput and what Suetonius says of Domitian.[48] Swift's purpose was to create a paradigm of royal cruelty that would apply as much to ancient as to modern tyrants.

About the only trait shared by George I and the King of Laputa is their common love of music. Nevertheless, the 'fundamental Law' of Laputa whereby 'neither the King nor either of his two elder Sons, are permitted to leave the Island; nor the Queen till she is past Child-bearing' (III. iii. 172) has been taken as a reflection on George I's obtaining the repeal of the part of the Act of Settlement that required the monarch to obtain parliamentary approval before leaving the country. Perhaps so. But we are given no indication that the King of Laputa has any desire to leave the island; he seems content in his world of music and mathematical speculation. The idea that a king should reside in his country is a commonplace, recommended (for example) by Machiavelli as one of the best ways of keeping a conquered kingdom.[49] In any case, Laputa is his court and royal domain, not his country; it is as though George I had been forbidden to leave St. James's or the Crown lands. Laputa is a court remote from its country, like Versailles. Swift is criticizing the law that keeps the king remote from his people, not using it to reflect on George I.[50]

---

[48] R. F. Kennedy, 'Swift and Suetonius', *Notes and Queries*, n.s. xvi (1969), 340-1. A similar anecdote is told about Septimius Severus, that after suppressing the revolt of Clodius Albinus he extolled his own mercy at the same time as he put numerous senators to death (*Scriptores Historiae Augustae*, Severus, xii. 9).

[49] *The Prince*, Chapter iii; *Works*, trans. Nevile (London, 1694), p. 200.

[50] Another supposed thrust at George I, the King of Laputa's 'being distinguished above all his Predecessors for his Hospitality to Strangers' (III. ii. 160-1), would apply to James I and William III at least as much as to George I. But it may

The difference between a 'portrait' of George I and a 'paradigm' of corrupt or tyrannical kingship can be seen by comparing the treatment of the King of Laputa with the character of Regoge in Swift's 'Account of the Court and Empire of Japan'. The narrative of the 'Account' is a transparent allegory of English history, and the character of Regoge incorporates most of Swift's reasons for dissatisfaction with George I (*P.W.* v. 101). To mistake the King of Laputa for an attack on George I is to confuse the nature of the satire and to place an unnecesary limitation on a general critique of contemporary kingship.

The general consensus with which critics have agreed in seeing George I in the Emperor of Lilliput and the King of Laputa contrasts strongly with the bewildering disagreement over the character of Munodi, the out-of-office statesman of Lagado (III. iv. 174–8). The only point of agreement about Munodi is that he must represent someone, and the ranks of Swift's contemporaries have been ransacked for likely candidates.[51] In discussing the claims of these contenders, it is pertinent first of all to note that, since Munodi is a flattering portrait (if it is indeed a portrait), there could be no conceivable reason for Swift to have disguised it. Even the most committed believer in the need for cautious, satiric indirection under the Walpole regime can hardly explain why it should have been necessary to disguise a complimentary portrait. Since there would be no reason for dissimulation, we might naturally expect to find a higher degree of resemblance between Munodi and his original than with the satiric portraits, where the argument for indirection may possibly have some force.

Munodi 'was a Person of the first Rank, and had been

---

be just an ironic comment, since Gulliver later complains of neglect (III. iv. 173).

[51] Bolingbroke was suggested by G. Ravenscroft Dennis, in his edition of *Gulliver's Travels* (London, 1899; vol. viii of the Temple Scott edition of Swift's *Prose Works*), p. 181. Support has come from Harold Williams in his edition (London, 1926), p. 479, and from Philip Mahone Griffith, 'Swift's Munodi and Bolingbroke, a Firmer Identification', *South Central Bulletin*, no. 36 (Winter 1976), 145–6. Midleton was put forward by Firth, *Essays*, p. 239, and has recently attracted support from Downie, 'Political Characterization', pp. 116–17. Oxford is the candidate of Case, *Four Essays*, pp. 87–9. Robert C. Steensma, 'Swift's Model for Lord Munodi', *Notes and Queries*, n.s. xii (1965), 216–17, argues for Sir William Temple.

some Years Governor of *Lagado*; but by a Cabal of Ministers was discharged for Insufficiency. However the King treated him with Tenderness, as a well-meaning Man, but of a low contemptible Understanding' (III. iv. 175). Munodi is a symbol of conservatism and opposition to the spirit of the Academy of Lagado, as shown in the episode of the mill (III. iv. 177–8). Munodi has the most detailed political biography of any of the political characters in *Gulliver's Travels*. If he had an original, he should not be difficult to find. But the right combination proves surprisingly elusive, as the number of rival contenders testifies.

The least likely candidate is Lord Midleton, who was Lord Chancellor of Ireland at the time of Wood's halfpence. But although he was a firm opponent of the patent itself, he was a stauch assertor of the rightness of the English domination of Ireland. He supported the prosecution of the Drapier, and declined the dedication of the collected edition of the *Drapier's Letters*. There is enough here to disqualify him, but a glance at some incidents in his earlier career shows how obnoxious he would have been to Swift. He was a Whig creature who supported an extension of toleration and a repeal of the Test Act in Ireland. Swift regarded the Test Act as the Irish Church's great bulwark against creeping dissent. In 1707 Midleton had even gone to England to suggest a repeal of the Test Act by the English parliament. It is clear from a letter of 1720 that Swift regarded him as a placeman and time-server (*Corr*. ii. 358). There is no evidence that Swift admired his character. Rather the contrary, for the tone of the letter addressed to Midleton is cool to the point of suppressed hostility (*P.W.* x. 99–115). Swift welcomes Midleton as a temporary ally in the fight against Wood, all the more valuable for being unexpected. If even court sycophants like Midleton are against the patent, there must be something wrong with it. Midleton could not possibly have had anything to do with Munodi.

Temple, Oxford, and Bolingbroke are all more plausible and attractive candidates than Midleton, for Swift did at least have a genuine admiration for them. But in no case are the parallels exact enough to suggest that he was thinking of any one of them when he drew the character and sketched the career of Munodi. Temple's character and conservatism are close enough to Munodi's, but he never held the same kind of office and he was never discharged by a cabal. On the contrary, he was repeatedly offered and declined high office. Nor is there anything in his career that can even remotely have suggested the incident of the mill. With Oxford, the difficulties are the reverse: there are parallels of career, but not of character. Swift knew Oxford well, and although he admired him as a man he deplored the brand of politics he practised, with its scheming, mysteries, and refinement (*P.W.* viii. 80-1). The accusation of having a 'low contemptible Understanding' must be translated to mean that Munodi had plain, common, good sense. That was never Oxford's failing. Similar objections apply to Bolingbroke. There are parallels of career, but hardly of character. Swift in 1714 had been attracted by Bolingbroke's more extreme Tory policies, but had reservations about his character. Even when he could see that Oxford's power was sinking, he preferred retirement to the country to joining wholeheartedly Bolingbroke's faction. And, unlike Pope, he seems never to have been taken in by Bolingbroke's cant about his happiness and content with a life of 'Study and Retirement' (*Corr.* ii. 461-2). Writing to Pope, but replying in effect to letters from both Pope and Bolingbroke singing the praises of retirement, Swift commented tartly 'I have no very strong Faith in you pretenders to retirement' (20 September 1723; *Corr.* ii. 464).

None of the suggested candidates is sufficiently like Munodi in career and character to be regarded as his 'original'. Munodi is a paradigm of the benevolent, conservative, country gentleman of Swift's Tory mythology (the equivalent at his level of society of the King of Brobdingnag), ready to serve his country in a political post, but as ready to retire and to rest content in a private station. Munodi's career also illustrates Swift's belief in the likely fate of a man of principle and integrity in the dirty world of contemporary politics. The fact that Munodi's post (Governor of Lagado) had no exact equivalent in England was probaly intended as a hint not to search for a historical original, and, as elsewhere, the multiplicity of candidates tends to argue against any one of them having been intended. Nevertheless, Swift may well have thought of Temple, Oxford, and Bolingbroke as in some particular ways exemplifying the paradigm of Munodi. In a letter to Bolingbroke, he sketches 'a romance of a great minister's life', and it is a curious amalgam of memories of Temple, Oxford, and Bolingbroke and wish-fulfilling fantasies of the future: 'he should begin it as Aristippus has done; then be sent into exile, and employ his leisure in writing the memoirs of his own administration; then be recalled, invited to resume his share of power, act as far as was decent; at last, retire to the country, and be a pattern of hospitality, politeness, wisdom, and virtue' (*Corr.* ii. 332). The date of the letter from which this passage is taken is 19 December 1719, about eighteen months before Swift began to write *Gulliver's Travels*. Already in the letter we can see the imaginative process of generalizing his experience that was shortly to lead to the creation of his masterpiece. The imaginary 'romance' takes off from the starting-point of the careers of men whom Swift has known (there may also be a hint of Clarendon writing his memoirs), but they are soon subsumed in the general paradigm.

This discussion, lengthy as it has been, has by no means exhausted the subject. I have said nothing, for example, about the King of Brobdingnag.[52] But it has not seemed necessary for my general argument to take issue with every identification of a character with a historical figure that has been proposed, or to counter, point by point, the detailed arguments put forward in favour of the examples I have taken up. In most cases, the very multiplicity of interpretation supports my case for general readings. The more one reads in satire of the period, the more one is struck by its explicitness when it has a particular target in view. Its authors tend to err rather on the side of making sure the reader knows what is going on than of supersubtlety.[53] The examples I

---

[52] Ehrenpreis, *The Personality of Jonathan Swift*, pp. 92–9, sees reflections of Sir William Temple in the King of Brobingnag. But the real significance of the connections that Ehrenpreis makes is to show how much Swift's Brobdingnag was influenced by Temple's ideas. The personal correlations Ehrenpreis draws are much less convincing.

[53] In another context, Irvin Ehrenpreis notes that 'even those Augustan poems that embody dangerous material—subversive politics, personal satire, irreligion— will often be found to include explicit or discursive passages to orient the reader and keep him from misunderstanding the argument' ('Explicitness in Augustan

have discussed suggest that nowhere in *Gulliver's Travels* are we compelled to accept a personal interpretation of the satire, and that, on the contrary, Swift's satiric points are usually enhanced by generalizing them as much as possible. The tradition of misreading personalities into the satire of *Gulliver's Travels* is as old as the work itself, and it has burgeoned rather than diminished with the passage of time. But common sense, if not critical ingenuity, suggests that Swift's characters and incidents reflect on kings, ministers, and factions in general, not on George I, Walpole, and the Whigs (only) in particular. In fact, they were almost as applicable to Queen Anne, Oxford, and the Tories. It would be merely reductive to suppose that Swift was only concerned with the petty political squabbles of his own time and country. It is a diversion of misplaced ingenuity to search for those ever elusive 'particular applications' that Gay spoke of. More important are Swift's general ideas and ideals.

Literature', in *Literary Meaning and Augustan Values*, Charlottesville, 1974, p. 5). The whole essay (pp. 1–48 in the book) is a necessary recall of criticism to sanity. It complements, from a different angle, my rejection of most of the over-ingenious interpretations of the politics of *Gulliver's Travels*.

CHAPTER 5

The Politics of Common Sense

'I find no considerable man very angry at the book', Pope wrote to Swift shortly after the publication of *Gulliver's Travels*, 'some indeed think it rather too bold, and too general a Satire: but none that I hear of accuse it of particular reflections' (*Corr.* iii. 181). Pope's comments were echoed by Gay: 'The Politicians to a man agree, that it is free from particular reflections, but that the Satire on general societies of men is too severe' (*Corr.* iii. 182). Replying to Pope about a month later, Swift wrote that in Ireland readers' reactions had been rather different: 'some think it wrong to be so hard upon whole Bodies or Corporations, yet the general opinion is, that reflections on particular persons are most to be blamed' (*Corr.* iii. 189). Since this comes from the letter in which Swift refers to the sceptical Irish bishop and keeps up a pretence of not having written *Gulliver*, it is difficult to know how to take his statement. Possibly he was just intent on emphasizing how wrong and perverse Irish reactions had been. At all events, it seems clear that Swift, Pope, and Gay themselves all regarded readings of *Gulliver's Travels* that emphasized 'particular reflections' as wrong-headed or misguided, while they better understood readers who found the satire too severe on 'general societies of men'. George I, they knew, was only an example of a certain kind of kingship; Walpole himself mattered less than the institution of a prime minister. At the heart of the critique of politics and society in *Gulliver's Travels* was not personal satire but an indictment of how societies and their institutions became corrupt and degenerate.

Gulliver's French translator, the Abbé Desfontaines, had written in his preface that, 'Il est clair que ce Livre n'a point été écrit pour la France, mais pour l'Angleterre, & que ce qu'il renferme de satyre particuliere & directe ne nous touche point.'[1] But when he wrote to Swift after his translation had

---

[1] *Voyages de Gulliver* (Paris, 1727), i. xxxv. This passage was allowed to stand

been well received and had gone into a second edition, Desfontaines tried tactfully to gloss over the criticisms that he had made in his original preface (*Corr.* iii. 217). It is not clear whether Desfontaines was genuinely apologizing to his readers for what he thought was a limitation of *Gulliver's Travels*, or trying to cover himself in advance against the possible charge of satirizing his own monarchy, court, and government. Certainly Swift replied with an uncompromising claim for at least a European relevance for *Gulliver*:

si donc les livres du Sieur Gulliver ne sont calcules que pour les Isles Britanniques, ce voyageur doit passer pour un tres pitoyable Ecrivain. Les memes vices, et les memes follies regnent par tout, du moins, dans tous les pays civilises de l'Europe, et l'auteur qui n'ecrit que pour une ville, une province, un Royaume, ou meme un siecle, merite si peu d'être traduit qu'il ne merite pas d'etre lû.   (*Corr.* iii. 226.)

This European relevance is worth insisting on, because modern commentators have been too ready to limit the satire in *Gulliver's Travels* not only to 'particular applications' but to particular English applications. Naturally Swift drew most for illustrations on the country whose society and history he knew best, but France is the next most important source (whatever Desfontaines may have thought) and Swift drew on the whole of his historical knowledge, of ancient Rome and Renaissance Italy as well as modern England and France.

Swift was able to do this with no sense of incongruity because of his approach to history: political forms might change, political follies remained the same.[2] But his view of history was not so simple as to assume that all societies at all times could be analysed in the same way. His uniformitarianism was combined with a cyclical view of history. Both ideas were extremely widely held at the time, notably by Swift's friends and political sympathizers, Pope and Bolingbroke.[3] They all three saw contemporary Europe, and England in particular, as having entered a period of decline. As in the early days of the Roman Empire, luxury and tyranny had resulted in corruption, degeneration, and decay. But cyclic

---

in the second edition, but a passage listing the faults of the book (pp. xv–xvi) was considerably toned down.

[2] See above, pp. 33–6.

[3] See Isaac Kramnick, *Bolingbroke and His Circle* (Cambridge, Mass., 1968).

theories of history allow for the possibility of reform and improvement, and it is notable that in *Gulliver's Travels* Swift by no means confines his interest to societies in decline. Instead he depicts them at various stages of cyclic development. Lilliput is a well-established tyranny, Brobdingnag a well-balanced mixed government. Laputa–Balnibarbi seems to be, at the time Gulliver visits it, in a state of incipient disintegration.[4] Similarly, in contemporary Europe, different national states were at different stages of constitutional development. Thus it was appropriate for Swift, trying to give *Gulliver's Travels* a permanent European relevance, to depict societies that would represent not particular European states but rather types of states.

Unlike Harrington in *Oceana* (or even More in *Utopia*), in *Gulliver's Travels* Swift largely avoided any systematic exposition of political or institutional analysis. Instead, his political ideas are incorporated into a more elaborate narrative fiction than More's or Harrington's. As a result, however, we know far less about Swift's imaginary societies and what information we are given is often attended with difficulties of interpretation. We do not have much difficulty in *Utopia* in working out where More stands on particular questions, or why he describes particular customs and ideas. But with *Gulliver's Travels* we do not always know which details are supposed to be significant, and which are to be taken rather as jokes, as local colour, or as authenticating detail intended to lend an air of verisimilitude.[5] Thus in Lilliput, commentators have sought to relate the disused Temple in which Gulliver lives to some external circumstances, but not Gulliver's watch. Yet Gulliver had to have somewhere to stay, while his watch receives attention far beyond its narrative function. Does it satirize modern man's habit of scurrying about, like the White Rabbit, perpetually in fear of missing some appointment? Or does it refer to some particular man noted for the mannerism of always pulling out his watch? Almost certainly not, yet

---

[4] Houyhnhnmland, by contrast, illustrates the common idea that the happiest people has no history.

[5] This problem is raised (although not solved) in Frank Brady, 'Vexations and Diversions: Three Problems in *Gulliver's Travels*', *Modern Philology*, lxxv (1978), 346–67.

these conjectures are as plausible as the suggestions that have been made about the Temple. Again, why should the incident of Flimnap's fall on to one of the king's cushions (I. iii. 39) be more significant than Gulliver's own near-fall prevented by the governess's corking-pin (II. v. 121)?

There are also many subjects of legitimate interest to students of Gulliverian political institutions that Swift simply glosses over or says nothing about. For example, surprisingly little attention is paid to the machinery of representative government: to parliaments, elections, corruption, and bribery. This was not due to fear of prosecution, for what incidental references there are (e.g. III. viii. 202) reflect directly on the British situation. The explanation seems to be that Swift, for all his belief in balanced government, was not particularly interested in the workings of parliament as an institution. References to parliament in the *Journal to Stella* suggest that Swift saw its role as following the lead of some able and disinterested statesman. He had no belief in its ability to do anything on its own.[6] Another subject that Swift deliberately avoided was religion. Here the reason seems to have been that Swift felt that any treatment of substantive religious issues and differences would blunt the impact of his political satire. Thus in Part I the schism is about an inessential of form, and in Part II the Brobdingnagians are even polytheistic (II. iv. 114).

Swift's major interests in *Gulliver's Travels* were 'high' politics (the world of kings, courts, and ministers) and the political infrastructure (law, education, and learning). The rationale behind these emphases is not far to seek. Parts of *Gulliver's Travels* were certainly intended as serious contributions to current debates on political issues. Swift (unlike the Gulliver of the 'Letter to Sympson') did not expect major reforms within six months or less. What he did expect, and he was not unreasonable in doing so, was that a change of

---

[6] In March 1711, 'the Parliament at present cannot go a step without him, nor the queen' (*J.S.* i. 205); when Harley was to be made a peer Swift commented that 'they will want him prodigiously in the House of Commons, of which he is the great mover, and after him the secretary, and hardly any else of weight' (*J.S.* i. 249); after Harley's elevation, St. John is 'much the greatest Commoner in Engld, and turns the whole Parlmt, who can do nothing without him' (*J.S.* ii. 495).

monarch or government might affect the whole direction of the country's politics. He had seen it happen on Harley's assumption of power in 1710, and again on the fall of the Tories in 1714. In 1726 he might hope for a radical change for the better if George I dismissed Walpole (as he was rumoured to intend) in favour of Bolingbroke, or when the Prince of Wales came to the throne. Such occurrences were frequent in Europe: the deaths of Louis XIV in 1715 and Charles XII in 1718 had resulted in major realignments of national policies. If substantial political change were to come, it would most likely come from the top. Swift would hardly have conceived the possibility of political change engineered from below, and if it had occurred to him it could only have appeared sinister and deplorable. Hence the attention paid in *Gulliver's Travels*, seemingly excessive to the modern reader, to the courts and characters of kings.

/ Swift believed that a king should be the symbolic father of his country and that his court should correspondingly be domestic rather than pompous in character. Throughout *Gulliver's Travels*, the physical descriptions of the various courts are emblematic. In centralized and absolutist Lilliput the royal palace is at the centre of the capital city. The three concentric courts suggest the isolation in which the Emperor lives (I. iv. 46–7). By contrast, the King of Brobdingnag's palace is 'no regular Edifice, but an Heap of Buildings' (II. iv. 112).[7] In Lilliput the atmosphere of the court is one of intrigue; in Brobdingnag, of thoughtful and serious domesticity. In Laputa, the court's isolation on the Flying Island makes the point even more graphically that courts should not fly above but be integral parts of the countries they govern.

A virtuous ruler might effect a temporary change of direction, but any more permanent improvement in the political life of a society would have to come about as a result of changes in national education and political culture. Hence the interest and attention given to such matters in *Gulliver's Travels*. Such changes could only be imposed from above. A virtuous and rational ruler might stem the tide of corruption and prepare for many generations of more orderly and stable

[7] French visitors to London were regularly struck by how unimpressive Kensington Palace was compared to Versailles.

political life by establishing better social institutions. These would in turn be subject to decay and degeneration, and the cycle would begin anew. But the task of the public-spirited ruler or citizen was clear: in times of virtue, to preserve what was good for as long as possible againt corruption; in times of corruption, to work for a renewal of what was amiss. Because *Gulliver's Travels* was calculated for more than contemporary England in a particular phase of decline, Swift allows for multiple possibilities. Thus while his general values are stability, hierarchy, and paternalism in government, he shows both a society in which the actual need is for less authority (Lilliput), one which needs more than it has (Laputa), and one which is balanced approximately correctly (Brobdingnag). To readers in contemporary Poland, it would have appeared that in offering Brobdingnag as a model Swift was recommending stronger central government. To readers in contemporary France, he would have seemed to be recommending a weaker central executive. Readers in England might have had the vanity to suppose that England had achieved the Brobdingnagian balance.[8]

Apart from the Emperors of Blefuscu and Japan, whose brief roles in Parts I and III are largely functional, Swift depicts monarchs of four types, ranging from the most absolute to the relatively limited. The most despotic is the King of Luggnagg, the atmosphere of whose court is reminiscent of seventeenth-century travellers' accounts of oriental kingdoms like Siam, where subjects remained prostrate in the presence of a king who possessed absolute power of life and death. In a spell of bad weather in the summer of 1722 Swift read 'I know not how many diverting Books of History and Travells' at Loughall, the home of his friend Robert Cope (*Corr.* ii. 430). No doubt this reading influenced *Gulliver's Travels* in a general way, especially the parts of the work that parody travel writing. The King of Luggnagg is a parody of

---

[8] See, for example, the panegyric on the perfection of the British constitution in *The Third Charge of Sir Daniel Dolins, Kt., to the Grand-Jury and Other Juries of the County of Middlesex* (London, 1726). W. A. Speck, *Stability and Strife* (London, 1977), p. 20, suggests that Gulliver's mock-praise of the constitution to the King of Brobdingnag (II. vi. 127–9) is a parody of the excesses of Dolins and his kind.

oriental kingship rather than a serious critique of European despotism.

The extreme deference paid to oriental rulers is parodied in the form of Gulliver's application for an audience: he has to 'desire that his Majesty would please to appoint a Day and Hour, when it would be his gracious Pleasure that I might have the Honour to *lick the Dust before his Footstool*' (III. ix. 204). There is something of the same oriental character about the Emperor of Lilliput, whose dress is 'between the *Asiatick* and the *European*' (I. ii. 30) and whose preposterous style of titles (I. iii. 43) is likewise more extravagant than that of the kings of Europe.[9] But if the Emperor's titles are a joke, his powers certainly are not. Despite his character as 'a renowned Patron of Learning' (I. i. 26), the Emperor is excessively ambitious, intolerant, an intriguer, and the head of a faction more than he is the father of his country. There is no need to suppose that the reference to his patronage of learning is ironic, for the absolute princes of Europe (foremost among them Louis XIV) had a good record in this respect. But the Emperor also resembles Louis XIV in his ambitions to establish a universal monarchy. On Gulliver's capture of the Blefuscan fleet, 'he seemed to think of nothing less than reducing the whole Empire of *Blefuscu* into a Province, and governing it by a Viceroy; of destroying the *Big-Endian* Exiles and compelling that People to break the smaller End of their Eggs; by which he would remain sole Monarch of the whole World' (I. v. 53). This is comic enough when we remember that his dominions 'extend five Thousand Blustrugs, (about twelve Miles in Circumference) to the Extremities of the Globe' (I. iii. 43). But untold numbers of real human lives had been sacrificed for the similar ambitions of Ninus, Philip of Macedon, and most recently Louis XIV (for their association, see *P.W.* i. 202, 208).

One respect in which the character and actions of the

---

[9] The titles of the Emperor of Lilliput seem to be loosely a parody of those of eastern princes. A splendid example is the style of the Turkish Sultan, which can be found at the opening of an ambassador's letter of introduction appended to *The Four Epistles of A. G. Busbecquius concerning his Embassy into Turkey* (English translation, London, 1694), pp. 414–15. This was a popular travel book, and Swift may have read it.

Emperor reflect on George I is his factionalism. He is a monarch of 'Schemes and Politicks' (I. v. 53). In one of his 'Thoughts on Various Subjects' Swift describes 'Politicks, as the Word is commonly understood' as 'nothing but Corruptions; and consequently of no Use to a good King, or a good Ministry: For which Reason, Courts are so over-run with Politicks' (*P.W.* iv. 246-7). The Emperor has 'determined to make use of only low Heels in the Administration of the Government, and all Offices in the Gift of the Crown' (I. iv. 48). Swift never forgot the opportunity that he thought George I had neglected, on his accession, of reconciling parties by forming a mixed administration (*P.W.* v. 99-100). But George I was not the only offender. The Catholic kings of Europe were even less tolerant than their Protestant counterparts. Louis XIV's revocation of the Edict of Nantes in 1685 was followed by a more intensive persecution of the Huguenots than anything known in England even after the severe anti-Catholic legislation enacted after 1688.[10] In Book IV of the *Laws*, Plato had described how 'after a contest for office, the victorious side engrosses the conduct of public affairs so completely to itself that no share whatsoever of office is left to the vanquished, or even to their descendents' (715a). The Emperor of Lilliput represents not George I but the vices and failings of a whole class of arbitrary monarchs.

The nature of the Flying Island and the intense speculative preoccupations that he shares with his courtiers seem to remove the King of Laputa from the realm of reality. Nevertheless, while allowing for an element of playful fantasy, we are intended to recognize this monarch as an illustration of

[10] The main anti-Catholic penalties regularly enforced were the exclusion from civil office (shared by the Dissenters) and the double land tax. Other measures, such as those which forbade Catholics to live in London, to own arms and ammunition or a horse worth more than £5, or (from 1700) which made them incapable of inheriting or buying land, might be invoked in periods of crisis such as an invasion scare but would normally be allowed to sleep on the statute books. Few Catholics felt it necessary to leave the country on account of religious persecution. It was far otherwise in France, as the large number of Huguenot refugees testifies. No English Catholic had anything to fear like the dragonnade, or the chance of being condemned to the galleys. Catholic gentry could profess their religion and still enjoy security and even a modest prosperity; see the chapters on John Caryll in Howard Erskine-Hill, *The Social Milieu of Alexander Pope* (New Haven, 1975), pp. 42-102.

the need for practical restraints on royal power. He 'would be the most absolute Prince in the Universe, if he could but prevail on a Ministry to join with him' (III. iii. 171). But the paragraphs that follow indicate how his power is in fact limited: by his ministers' concern for their estates in Balnibarbi below, and by the danger to the Flying Island itself of trying to reduce rebellions by too severe a show of force. Thus in practice a working compromise is maintained: the people 'understand how far to carry their Obstinancy, where their Liberty or Property is concerned', and the king in his turn knows how far he can go (III. iii. 172). But the chaos that prevails on Balnibarbi below, and the feverish unreality of life on the Flying Island, make it clear how uneasy a compromise it is.

The main point of Swift's criticism of the king is based on a Renaissance ideal of kingship (represented in *Gulliver's Travels* by the King of Brobdingnag) in which the king would have an intelligent and informed interest in the whole world of the mind, not an overspecialized interest in some few subjects. Among examples of princes whose intellectual interests caused them to neglect the business of government would be the Emperor Rudolf II and the Elector of Cologne. The Elector's particular interest was chemistry. Sir William Temple refers to him in his 1671 'Survey' of Europe,[11] and Swift may have heard anecdotes of him from Temple. The King of Laputa may also be intended to satirize, in a good-natured way, the rather formidable mathematical training that Plato prescribes for his ruling élite in Book VII of the *Republic*.

It is only in Brobdingnag that we meet a king whose powers are circumscribed not by necessity but by conviction. This 'Prince possessed of every Quality which procures Veneration, Love and Esteem; of strong Parts, great Wisdom and profound Learning; endued with admirable Talents for Government, and almost adored by his Subjects' (II. vii. 135) indignantly rejects Gulliver's offer of the secret of gunpowder.[12] The terms

---

[11] *Miscellanea* (London, 1680), p. 10.

[12] The king's magnanimous scorn of Gulliver's proposal to make him absolute contrasts with historical examples. Tacitus describes the hypocrisy with which, on the death of Augustus, Tiberius pretended reluctance to accept the imperial power

in which the King of Brobdingnag is presented offer a complete contrast to the Emperor of Lilliput. Emphasis is placed on his qualities of mind: he is 'as learned a Person as any in his Dominions' (II. iii. 103) and 'a Prince of excellent Understanding' (II. vi. 127). He is a good family man, as evidenced by his weekly dinners *en famille* (II. iii. 106). He is a lover of peace (II. vi. 131). The Emperor of Lilliput had been a patron of learning, but he was personally warlike and given to intrigue. The King of Brobdingnag is a man of wide general knowledge and broad principles (ironically mistaken by Gulliver as *'narrow Principles* and *short Views'*, (II. vii. 135)). His intelligent questioning of Gulliver reveals not only a naturalist's interest in a strange new species, but a shrewd moral understanding of human nature and its corruptions. He is, as a king should be, 'a Prince of much Gravity, and austere Countenance' (II. iii. 103). He is above faction, and above personal ambition. He is, as he desires to be, not the master but the father of his country. His rule illustrates the felicity that might follow from the conjunction of 'political power and philosophical intelligence' that Plato imagined in the *Republic* (473d).

The politics of the King of Brobdingnag, like Swift's own, are the politics of common sense. When Gulliver tells the king that 'there were several thousand Books among us written upon the Art of Government', the king is not impressed:

He professed both to abominate and despise all *Mystery, Refinement,* and *Intrigue,* either in a Prince or a Minister. He could not tell what I meant by *Secrets of State,* where an Enemy or some Rival Nation were not in the Case. He confined the Knowledge of governing within very *narrow Bounds;* to common Sense and Reason, to Justice and Lenity, to the Speedy Determination of Civil and criminal Causes; with some other obvious Topicks which are not worth considering.   (II. vi. 135.)

It is often overlooked that these implied strictures on English and European politics are almost equally applicable to what Swift saw as the failings of the Tory administration of 1710–14 as to the Whig ministries under George I. Swift's first-hand

---

(*Annals*, i. 11–12). In Molesworth's account of the establishment of absolutism in Denmark, he stresses the king's pretended unwillingness but strongly implies that the whole affair was stage-managed by him; *An Account of Denmark as It Was in the Year 1692* (London, 1694), pp. 56–7, 65.

experience of the '*Mystery, Refinement*, and *Intrigue*' of Oxford's methods certainly reinforced his bias in favour of the politics of common sense. In 'Some Free Thoughts upon the Present State of Affairs' (written in May 1714, although not published until 1741) he is particularly critical of Oxford's lack of straightforwardness. He begins with a statement of principle that anticipates the King of Brobdingnag:

God has given the Bulk of Mankind a Capacity to understand Reason when it is fairly offered; and by Reason they would easily be governed, if it were left to their Choice. Those Princes in all Ages who were most distinguished for their mysterious Skill in Government, found by the Event that they had ill consulted their own Quiet, or the Ease and Happiness of their People; neither hath Posterity remembered them with Honour.   (*P.W.* viii. 77.)

The examples Swift cites are Lysander, Philip of Macedon, Tiberius, Louis XI, Pope Alexander VI, Cesare Borgia, Catherine de' Medici, and Philip II of Spain. He then applies the same principle to ministers without naming any examples, but it becomes clear as the pamphlet progresses that it is Oxford that he has chiefly in mind.

The point of Swift's citation of Lysander and the other examples is well illustrated by the parallels of character and career that he would have observed between Lysander and Oxford. On the credit side, both were men of unusual financial probity. In his 'Life' of Lysander, Plutarch noted that although he enriched Sparta, 'from the vast wealth and power in his hands . . . he had not, even in the slightest degree, sought to amass money for the aggrandizement of his family' (xxx). Swift says of Oxford that 'his Liberality and Contempt of Money were such, that he almost ruined his Estate while he was in Employment; Yet his Avarice for the Public was so great, that it neither consisted with the present Corruptions of the Age, nor the Circumstances of the Time' (*P.W.* viii. 136). In this respect Oxford was the opposite of Marlborough and (later) Walpole. But Lysander's political, diplomatic, and military methods were (like Oxford's) often scheming and indirect. Plutarch comments that 'to those who loved simplicity and nobility in the characters of their leaders, Lysander, compared with Callicratidas, seemed to be unscrupulous and subtle, a man who tricked out most of what he did in war with the varied hues of deceit' (vii). Lysander's deep-laid plot to reform the Spartan constitution (xxiv-xxv) was frustrated by his unexpected death, so that all his schemes came ultimately to nothing. Swift deplored the schemings and refinements of Oxford's politics, and his attitude was confirmed by their failure. As the examples cited in 'Some Free Thoughts' showed, such politics were rarely successful.

In a pamphlet written in 1715, although not published until 1765, Swift returned to the theme of the politics of common sense: 'God intending the Government of a Nation in the severall Branches and Subordinations of Power, hath made the Science of Governing sufficiently obvious to common Capacities; otherwise the world would be left in a desolate Condition, if great Affairs did always require a great Genius, whereof the most fruitfull Age will hardly produce above three or four in a Nation' (*P.W.* viii. 138). This conviction was to find its way into the original constitution of Lilliput, where 'they believe that the common Size of human Understandings, is fitted to some Station or other; and that Providence never intended to make the Management of publick Affairs a Mystery, to be comprehended only by a few Persons of sublime Genius, of which there seldom are three born in an Age' (I. vi. 59).[13]

The most complete contrast to this commonsensical ideal shared by Swift, the King of Brobdingnag, and the original framers of the Lilliputian constitution is offered by the actual state of affairs in Lilliput at the time of Gulliver's visit and for some generations previously. Lilliputian politics are conducted in an atmosphere of secrecy, mystery, caballing, and intrigue. Indirection is the preferred mode. Thus Gulliver learns a scrap of information from 'a particular Friend, a Person of great Quality, who was as much in the *Secret* as

---

[13] Trenchard and Gordon make the same point in *Cato's Letters*: 'there are not such mighty Talents requisite for Government, as some, who pretend to them without possessing them, would make us believe: Honest Affections, and common Qualifications, are sufficient; and the Administration has been always best executed, and the publick Liberty best preserved, near the Origin and Rise of States, when plain Honesty and common Sense alone governed the publick Affairs, and Men's Morals were not corrupted with Riches and Luxury, nor their Understandings perverted by Subtleties and Distinctions' (collected edition, London, 1723-4, i. 182). This is one of many Swiftian passages in *Cato's Letters.*

any' (I. ii. 32). Skyresh Bolgolam 'was pleased, without any Provocation, to be my mortal Enemy' (I. iii. 42) and engages in a personal feud with Gulliver. Subsequently Gulliver has to contend with other 'secret Enemies' (I. v. 53), with a 'Junta of Ministers' (I. v. 54), and 'the Malice of my Enemies' (I. v. 55). A 'private Intrigue' is formed against him, and council meetings are called 'in the most private Manner' on his account (I. vii. 67). There is a certain comedy in the absurdly elaborate precautions taken by these enemies, but the clear implication is that the Lilliputians are subject to the same or worse treatment.

A similar topsy-turvydom is evident in Part III, where Munodi, who seems about the most sensible man in Balnibarbi (and thus by Swift's own criteria the best fitted for the exercise of political power) 'had been some Years Governor of *Lagado*; but by a Cabal of Ministers was discharged for Insufficiency' (III. iv. 175). In the political wing of the Academy of Lagado there is a professor particularly skilled in 'discovering Plots and Conspiracies against the Government' (III. vi. 190). His method is highly indirect, based not on overt actions but on investigations of diet and digestive processes. Gulliver himself makes a notable contribution to the subject, adding ciphers and anagrams as means of discovering well-hidden plots (III. vi. 190-2). In this passage on plots Swift had in mind not only the recent tactics of the Whigs in connection with Gyllenborg in 1716-17 and Atterbury in 1722-3, but earlier practicioners of the same art such as Nero, Domitian, and the Borgias.

An aspect of government in which Swift particularly interested himself during his days of influence under the Tory government was the proper use and distribution of government patronage. At first at least, Swift was able to rise above party considerations: his efforts on behalf of certain deserving Whig place-holders like Congreve are well attested. Even at the height of party animosities, Swift retained a bias in favour of people who were qualified. He never lost a certain *naïvety* about the way politics and political patronage actually worked, and seems to have been genuinely surprised at how often ministers (including those he otherwise admired) preferred to reward dependable mediocrity rather than men of

ability. His own modest preferment as Dean of St. Patrick's
is a case in point. In a letter to Edward Harley in 1720 he
prided himself that 'in disposing of these Musical Emplymts
I determine to act directly contrary to Ministers of State, by
giving them to those who best deserve' (*Corr.* ii. 339). In
1725 he congratulated Carteret on occasionally rewarding
merit, unlike 'most great Men I have known these thirty Years
past, whom I have always observed to act as if they never
received a true Character, nor had any Value for the Best,
and consequently dispensed their Favours without the least
Regard to Abilities or Virtue. And this Defect I have often
found among those from whom I least expected it' (*Corr.* iii.
71-2). This problem is much discussed in *Gulliver's Travels*.
In Lilliput as originally constituted, 'in chusing Persons for
all Employments, they have more Regard to Morals than to
great Abilities' (I. vi. 59). But in present-day Lilliput candidates for employments and honours are tested only in rope-
dancing, leaping, and creeping (I. iii. 38-9). In Laputa, music
and mathematics are the essential qualifications. The 'great
Lord at Court' who had 'performed many eminent Services
for the Crown, had great natural and acquired Parts, adorned
with Integrity and Honour' is condemned to obscurity and
contempt for his deficiencies in the two essentials (III. iv.
173). One of the projects discussed in the Academy of
Lagado is that candidates should 'raffle for Employments'
(III. vi. 190), a method that would at least give the qualified
an equal chance with the unqualified.

At the magician's house in Glubbdubdrib, Gulliver speaks
with three kings who explain that 'in their whole Reigns they
did never once prefer any Person of Merit, unless by Mistake
or Treachery of some Minister in whom they confided:
Neither would they do it if they were to live again; and they
shewed with great Strength of Reason, that the Royal Throne
could not be supported without Corruption; because, that
positive, confident restive Temper, which Virtue infused into
Man, was a perpetual Clog to publick Business' (III. viii.
199-200). The openness of the avowal puts one in mind of
Walpole, and anticipates the speech Swift was soon to put
into his mouth in the guise of Lelop-Aw in the 'Account of
the Court and Empire of Japan' (1728; *P.W.* v. 104-7). But

the policy itself was just as characteristic of Oxford. The typical 'prime minister' that Gulliver describes to his Houy-hnhnm master in Part IV recalls Oxford even more than Walpole: 'Those he speaks worst of behind their Backs, are in the surest way to Preferment; and whenever he begins to praise you to others or to your self, you are from that Day forlorn. The worst Mark you can receive is a *Promise*, especially when it is confirmed with an Oath; after which every wise Man retires, and gives over all Hopes' (IV. vi. 255). In 'An Enquiry into the Behaviour of the Queen's Last Ministry' Swift noted of Oxford that 'some of us used to observe, that those whom he talked well of, or suffered to be often near him, were not in a Scituation of much Advantage; and that his mentioning others with Contempt or Dislike, was no Hindrance at all to their Preferment' (*P.W.* viii. 138). In the passage where the Lagadan projector proposes efficacious methods of curing the 'short and weak Memories' that princes and favourites are commonly troubled with (III. vi. 188), Swift likewise had in mind his own frustrating experiences with the delays and procrastinations of Oxford.

One of the first casualties of the common-sense approach to politics advocated by the King of Brobdingnag, whether in England or Lilliput, would have been the divisive and irrational two-party system. If Swift himself at times succumbed to the rage of party, that should not be allowed to obscure his more considered and statesmanlike attitude toward it. In Lilliput the contrast between the high-heels and the low-heels, and the parallel religious schism between the big-endians and the little-endians (I. iv. 49–50) is surprisingly even. It is the absurd rancour of party and factional differences over things in their own nature indifferent that was the object of his satire. Gulliver finds the Laputan mathematicians 'passionately disputing every Inch of a Party Opinion' (III. ii. 164) and we find this as absurd as the King of Brobdingnag does the idea that 'such diminutive Insects' as Gulliver and his kind could dispute about Whig and Tory (II. iii. 106–7). By the time he wrote *Gulliver's Travels*, Swift had arrived at a more balanced attitude to his own earlier passionate commitment to the Tories. He could look back on those furious party contests in the same spirit as Marvell did on the factions of Renaissance

Italy. The Guelphs and Ghibellines were 'so *nonconformable*' that 'they took care to differ in the least circumstances of any humane action: and, as those that have the Masons Word, secretly discern one another; so in the peeling or cutting but of an Onion, a *Guelph* and *vice versa* would at first sight have distinguish'd a Ghibiline'.[14]

In Swift's conception of the ideal state the authority of a benevolent and paternal monarch would be balanced by a legislature consisting of landed proprietors who also officered a national militia. The key roles played in this scheme by the landowners and their militia can be traced back through the 'country' party ideology of late Restoration politics to Harrington and Machiavelli.[15] One of his 'Thoughts on Various Subjects' was that 'Law in a free Country, is, or ought to be the Determination of the Majority of those who have Property in Land' (*P.W.* iv. 245). In the *Drapier's Letters* (1724) Swift again defines law as '*the Will of the Majority of those who have the Propety in Land*' (*P.W.* x. 134). The independence of this landed legislature could be guaranteed only if it (and not the king or an oligarchy of nobles) controlled the national defence forces.

In *Gulliver's Travels* Swift does not give much attention to the legislature part of this combination, but the question of militias against standing armies does play a prominent part in the make-up of the contrasting imaginary societies. In Brobdingnag the ideal of a land-oriented society is suggested by the circumstances that Gulliver is discovered by a farmer, and the whole first chapter of Part II helps to create an image of a predominately rural society. The farmer himself is by no means idealized, but his way of living is approved (II. i. 89). More important, however, is the role of the Brobdingnagian militia. Unlike the Emperor of Lilliput, the King of Brobdingnag appears to have no standing troops, for 'when he goes abroad on solemn Days, he is attended for State by a Militia Guard of five hundred Horse' (II. iv. 115). When he comes to describe the militia as a whole, Gulliver's European

---

[14] *The Rehearsal Transpros'd*, ed. D. I. B. Smith (Oxford, 1971), pp. 34–5. Swift owned a copy of the first edition (London, 1672; no. 302 in the sale catalogue, marked as annotated) and refers to it admiringly (*P.W.* i. 5).

[15] See above, pp. 41–5.

prejudices lead him to question whether 'that may be called an Army which is made up of Tradesmen in the several Cities, and Farmers in the Country, whose Commanders are only the Nobility and gentry, without Pay or Reward'. The structure of command is related to the social hierarchy of the society as a whole: 'every Farmer is under the Command of his own Landlord, and every Citizen under that of the principal Men in his own City, chosen after the Manner of *Venice* by *Ballot*' (II. vii. 138). When Gulliver explains to the king about the large standing armies of Europe, the king is 'amazed to hear me talk of a mercenary standing Army in the Midst of Peace, and among a free People. He said, if we were governed by our own Consent in the Persons of our Representatives, he could not imagine of whom we were afraid, or against whom we were to fight' (II. vi. 131).

Swift makes the same point repeatedly in his other political writings. In the *Examiner* (no. 20, 21 December 1710) he uses the image of 'a Kingdom as a great Family, whereof the Prince is the Father; and it will appear plainly, that Mercenary Troops are only *Servants armed*' (*P.W.* iii. 41).[16] In 'Of Publick Absurdityes in England' (an unfinished collection of political maxims not published until 1765) Swift expounds the idea at length (*P.W.* v. 80). In his 'Letter to Pope' Swift directed the attack specifically to the standing army kept up by George I and the Whigs (*P.W.* ix. 31-2). In the same vein, the King of Brobdingnag asks 'what Business we had out of our own Islands, unless upon the Score of Trade or Treaty, or to defend the Coasts with our Fleet' and asks 'whether a private Man's House might not better be defended by himself, his Children, and Family; than by half a Dozen Rascals picked up at a Venture in the Streets, for small Wages, who might get an Hundred Times more by cutting their Throats' (II. vi. 131).[17]

The army and foreign policies of Lilliput illustrate the direct opposite of the maxims of Swift and the King of Brob-

---

[16] Robert C. Steensma, 'Swift on Standing Armies: A Possible Source', *Notes and Queries*, n.s. x (1963), 215-16, points out that Sir William Temple uses the same father–children–servants metaphor in 'An Essay upon the Original and Nature of Government', *Miscellanea* (London, 1680), pp. 70-2.

[17] On the standing army controversy, see Lois G. Schwoerer, '*No Standing Armies!*': *The Antiarmy Ideology in Seventeenth-Century England* (Baltimore, 1974), and H. T. Dickinson, *Liberty and Property* (London, 1977), pp. 104-7.

dingnag. As a diversion, the Emperor orders 'that Part of his Army, which quarters in and about his Metropolis' to march between Gulliver's legs. This 'Part' of the army consists of 3,000 foot and 1,000 cavalry (I. iii. 42). Earlier Gulliver has told us that 'this Prince lives chiefly upon his own Demesnes; seldom, except upon great Occasions raising any Subsidies upon his Subjects, who are bound to attend him in his Wars at their own Expence' (I. ii. 33). Despite this theory, the Emperor has a standing army and the country seems to be involved in a semi-permanent state of war with Blefuscu. At least three years of the Emperor's seven-year reign have been spent in hostilities, giving an ironic flavour to the phrase 'in great Felicity, and generally victorious' (I. ii. 30). For the causes of the war are quite irrational: the emperor's determination to impose the small-endian orthodoxy on the Blefuscans and his ambitions for a universal monarchy.

We find the same contrast between the legal as between the military institutions of Lilliput and Blefuscu. In Lilliput, there is an admirable framework corrupted by practice. The characteristic Lilliputian institutions embody corrections of what Swift saw as the defects of the English law. The Lilliputians reward as well as punish, and pay less regard to technical offences than to moral crimes like ingratitude. Fraud is treated as more serious than theft (I. vi. 58–60). In the *Examiner* (no. 38, 26 April 1711) Swift had suggested that fraud outran the laws against it because 'it rarely happens that Men are rewarded by the Publick for their Justice and Virtue . . . Whereas Fraud, where it succeeds, gives present Pay'. He gave as an example the Dyot case, anticipating the Emperor of Lilliput in his shock that 'the Aggravation of his Crime, proved to be the Cause that saved his Life; and the additional heightning Circumstance of betraying his Trust, was found to be a legal Defence' (*P.W.* iii. 137, 138). Richard Dyot, a Commissioner of the Stamped Paper, had been acquitted on the ground that his crime was only a breach of trust (*J.S.* i. 39). In Lilliput Gulliver 'was once interceding with the King for a Criminal who had wronged his Master of a great Sum of Money, which he had received by Order, and ran away with; and happening to tell his Majesty, by way of Extenuation, that it was only a Breach of Trust; the Emperor thought it monstruous in me to offer, as a Defence, the greatest Aggravation of the Crime' (I. vi. 58).

Unfortunately, as in other aspects of Lilliputian life, the reality is not in perfect accord with the theory. Gulliver's own experiences show how little benefit is derived from the best laws when executed by a corrupt administration. The Lilliputian legal code is also complicated by such arbitrary capital offences as 'to make water within the Precincts of the Palace' (I. v. 56). Such offences are also found in despotic Luggnagg, where 'it is capital for those who receive an Audience to spit or wipe their Mouths in his Majesty's Presence' (III. ix. 205). In Part IV Gulliver gives his Houyhnhnm master an even bleaker indictment of the condition of contemporary European law (IV. v. 248–50, vii. 261). Much the same points are probed by the searching questions that the King of Brobdingnag asks Gulliver in his attempt to penetrate behind the idealized account that Gulliver offers (II. vi. 130).

Yet despite the general preference that Swift unmistakably gives to Brobdingnag and its institutions, he evidently approves of certain features of Lilliputian society.[18] One such aspect is the Lilliputian system of hospitals for the old and diseased, and the consequent absence of beggars (I. vi. 63). The presence of beggars in Brobdingnag (II. iv. 112) may be a necessary result of a less bureaucratized society, but it remains none the less an evil. The problem in Lilliput, as Swift presents it, is that the most elaborate formal procedures fail to prevent the most flagrant injustices. Every stage of Gulliver's career leaves some trace in the Lilliputian archives. The lord who first harangues Gulliver produces 'his Credentials under the Signet Royal, which he applied close to mine Eyes' (I. i. 25). The Emperor issues an 'Imperial Commission' and 'Assignments upon his Treasury' for Gulliver's food (I. ii. 32, 33). As in other bureaucracies, nuisances are finally rewarded with attention: 'I had sent so many Memorials and Petitions for my Liberty, that his Majesty at length mentioned the Matter first in the Cabinet, and then in a full Council' (I. iii. 42). Gulliver receives his freedom with proper formal-

---

[18] In the same way, Swift admired certain French institutions (such as the Academy) without liking the French system of government as a whole.

ity in an imposing document (I. iii. 43-4). When he makes his preparations against Blefuscu, he is careful to tell us that he had a warrant for the necessary supplies (I. v. 51). When his fortunes turn, the formal articles of impeachment are added to his dossier (I. vii. 68-9). In no other part of the book is there so much paperwork. And despite it all, Gulliver is con-demned 'without the *formal Proofs required by the strict Letter of the Law*' (I. vii. 71). It may be fine for the beggars, but the machinery of a centralized society is too easily con-verted into an instrument for tyranny. Swift, like the King of Brobdingnag, believed that in general less government was likely to be better government.

The legal system of Brobdingnag is characterized by extreme simplicity and a lack of the kind of ambiguity that allows a dextrous lawyer to argue that black is white. 'No Law of that Country must exceed in Words the Number of Letters in their Alphabet . . . They are expressed in the most plain and simple Terms, wherein those People are not Mercur-ial enough to discover above one Interpretation. And, to write a Comment upon any Law, is a Capital Crime' (II. vii. 136). This capital crime seems better calculated for the public advantage than the arbitrary prohibitions of Lilliput and Luggnagg. The needless complexitites of legal systems are a perennial topic for satire, and a return to common sense and simplicity a constant demand of utopian political planners. 'The best rule as to your laws in general', Harrington wrote, 'is that they be few. Rome, by the testimony of Cicero, was best governed under those of the twelve tables . . . Solon made few, Lycurgus fewer laws; commonwealths have fewest at this day of all other governments.'[19] This last point may have been true in 1656 when Harrington wrote, but within a few years newly absolutist Denmark would challenge the claim. The apparent anomaly illustrates the way such govern-ments (like those of France and Lilliput) might embody occasional good institutions within a generally pernicious framework. In a generally unfavourable account of Denmark (which Swift knew; *Corr.* i. 129), Molesworth made an excep-tion of the new Danish legal system. Their laws 'for Justice,

[19] *Oceana*, in *Political Works*, ed. J. G. A. Pocock (Cambridge, 1977), p. 187.

Brevity, and Perspicuity . . . exceed all that I know in the World. They are grounded upon Equity, and are all contained in one Quarto Volume, written in the Language of the Country, with so much plainness, that no Man, who can write and read, is so ignorant, but he may presently understand his own Case, and plead it too if he pleases, without the Assistance of Counsel or Attorney.'[20] Molesworth goes on to make some important qualifications, but the idea of the single quarto volume would have appealed to Swift. In his 'Letter to Sympson' prefixed to the 1735 edition, Gulliver laments that he has not heard of '*Smithfield* blazing with Pyramids of Law-Books' (*P.W.* xi. 6). A single volume (possibly smaller than a quarto) might contain all that was of value in whole legal libraries.

Not that it was only law books that were multiplied needlessly. In the Preface to *A Tale of a Tub* Swift had satirized both the endless making of books and the endless apologies for making them (*P.W.* i. 27-8). Brobdingnag has few books as well as few laws. The king's library 'which is reckoned the largest, doth not amount to above a thousand Volumes' (II. vii. 136). Swift himself managed with fewer than seven hundred, despite a jesting reference in a letter of 1714 to his having 'sent over six Boxes with Books by long Sea . . . they are all old Books, and half of them very bad ones bought at Auctions only to make a shew as a Dean of St Patricks should' (*Corr.* ii. 31).[21] More seriously, in 1729, Swift wrote to Pope that 'a great Library always maketh me melancholy, where the best Author is as much squeezed, and as obscure, as a Porter at a Coronation' (*Corr.* iii. 330). By contrast, in Lilliput 'many hundred large Volumes have been published upon this Controversy' of the egg-breaking dispute (I. iv. 49). In Laputa the astronomers 'have written large Systems concerning the Stone' (III. iii. 170). At the Academy of Lagado there is even a mechanical frame for the mindless production of books (III. v. 182-4). When Gulliver tells the King of Brobdingnag of the 'several thousand Books among us written upon the *Art of Government*' it gives the king 'a very mean

[20] *An Account of Denmark*, pp. 232-3.
[21] For an account of Swift's library and his book-buying habits, see Harold Williams, *Dean Swift's Library* (Cambridge, 1932).

Opinion of our Understandings' (II. vii. 135). It is amusing to note that during the last years of Queen Anne, when almost everything became more or less a matter of party, the possession of more or fewer books was no exception. Oxford had a very large library, but he was known as a patron of learning and Swift describes himself as having undergone the mortification of being 'out-done by the Earl of Oxford in my own trade as a Scholar' (*P.W.* ix. 28). In the *Examiner* Swift says ironically of Bolingbroke that he 'hath clearly mistaken the true Use of *Books*, which he has thumbed and spoiled with Reading, when he ought to have multiplied them on his shelves' (*P.W.* iii. 80). The implied contrast is with Whigs like Sunderland, whom Swift describes in the *History of the Four Last Years of the Queen* as having an 'overgrown Library' and yet failing to use it to improve his understanding (*P.W.* vii. 9).

All the various elements that made up Swift's view of history are present in his fictional worlds. The imaginary institutions that he describes in *Gulliver's Travels*, like their European counterparts, are subject to the injurious effects of time. Human nature is the same in the various societies, but this essential similarity is modified by their being in different stages of the evolutionary cycles through which Swift thought all societies passed. The histories of the different countries illustrate Swift's cyclic conception of history and also his (and Sir William Temple's) favourite historical idea of the role of accident and trifling causes as the springs of 'great' events.

Lilliput has the most detailed history in *Gulliver's Travels*. It is related to Gulliver as an explanation of the threatened invasion from Blefuscu (I. iv. 48–50). Its two major strands are a religious schism and a factional struggle. The religious history of Lilliput has been read as an allegory of the English Reformation, but the details do not correspond closely enough for this to be convincing.[22] Swift knew that the Reformation was a momentous historical process in which many important issues were involved. The schism between Lilliput and Blefuscu involves only an indifferent issue, and

[22] *Gulliver's Travels*, ed. Arthur E. Case (New York, 1938), p. 37. The spurious continuation of *A Tale of a Tub* is an example of how a contemporary would actually have done what Case interprets Swift as doing; see above, p. 97.

it is more likely that Swift intended it to highlight the senseless disputes between sects about inessentials. Such disputes
were by no means an exclusively post-Reformation phenom-
enon. Similarly, the party disputes in Lilliput typify all such
factional quarrels, not just those in England between the
Whigs and the Tories. What is noteworthy about Lilliputian
history is the way it illustrates the gradual growth of corruption. It was the present emperor's great-grandfather whose
son cut his finger and who consequently issued the edict
about breaking eggs at the smaller end. It was this grandfather
who introduced rope-dancing as a qualification for employment. It was within the reign of the present emperor that the
disputes between the high-heels and the low-heels began.
Lilliput is roughly a composite European-type state in its
present degenerate condition. Its modern history typifies that
of post-Reformation Europe: senseless wars and disputes
about nothing important.

The history of Brobdingnag (like its legal system) is rather
simpler than Lilliput's. No exact account is given, by we are
told that:

in the Course of many Ages they have been troubled with the same
Disease, to which the whole Race of Mankind is Subject; the Nobility
often contending for Power, the People for Liberty, and the King for
absolute Dominion. All which, however happily tempered by the Laws
of that Kingdom, have been sometimes violated by each of the three
Parties; and have more than once occasioned Civil Wars, the last whereof was happily put an End to by this Prince's Grandfather in a general
Composition.   (II. vii. 138.)

We notice the contrast between royal grandfathers: the one
in Lilliput introduced rope-dancing, the one in Brobdingnag
a lasting 'general Composition'. Again, as in Lilliput there is
no exact allegory of English history but rather a generalized
account of a typical European state. If the present condition
of Lilliput suggested any particular country, it would be
France rather than England. The vagueness of the 'general
Composition' in Brobdingnag is deliberate. Swift wanted it to
represent an ideal of mixed or balanced government, not the
particular set of safeguards that had been adopted in England,
or the United Provinces, or Sweden.

Politics plays a smaller part in the history of Laputa,

although in this case the actual dates given may have some significance. The projecting mania is dated by Munodi 'about Forty Years ago' (III. iv. 176). Since Gulliver arrived in Lagado early in 1708, that would be about 1670. This may well refer specifically to the major scientific advances of the later seventeenth century. But more generally, the projecting mania is another manifestation of the 'restless Humor' whose workings Sir William Temple had described in his essay 'Of Popular Discontents'.[23] This humour had been the cause of revolutions in states from ancient Israel and Greece to modern England and France.

In Gulliver's visit to Glubbdubdrib, Swift opens a perspective on actual historical events that confirms from real examples what we have already learned from the imaginary societies, how human institutions are subject to decay (III. vii–viii. 195–202). He makes a particular point of remarking how soon the arbitrary government of Rome under the emperors was corrupted (III. viii. 200–1). The same point is made about modern history, and both family and national pride is exposed as sham. Part of the heading prefixed to Chapter vii is 'Ancient and Modern History Corrected' (III. vii. 197), and it is worth noticing just how Gulliver 'corrects' history. The process has a negative and a positive aspect. Swift is concerned to expose 'the Roguery and Ignorance of those who pretend to write *Anecdotes*, or secret History; who send so many Kings to their Graves with a Cup of Poison; will repeat the Discourse between a Prince and chief Minister, where no Witness was by; unlock the Thoughts and Cabinets of Embassadors and Secretaries of State; and have the perpetual Misfortune to be mistaken' (III. viii. 199). Swift's scepticism about 'secret history' derived from his own experience of being near the centre of affairs during Oxford's ministry. His emphasis on the question in *Gulliver's Travels* was part of his general campaign to discredit the idea of the 'mystery' of politics and to reinforce his own preference for a politics of common sense. In 'Some Free Thoughts on the Present State of Affairs' (written in 1714) he wrote that 'I could produce innumerable Instances from my own Memory

[23] See above, pp. 30–1.

and Observation, of Events imputed to the profound Skill and Address of a Minister, which in reality were either the meer Effects of Negligence, Weakness, Humour, Passion or Pride; or at best, but the Natural Course of Things left to themselves' (*P.W.* viii. 79).

Having demolished the pretended mystique of the professional politicians, Swift delights in exposing the 'real' causes. This had been a favourite pastime of Temple's. In 'An Enquiry into the Behaviour of the Queen's Last Ministry' (written in 1715) Swift refers approvingly to 'the common Observation of the greatest Events depending frequently upon the lowest, vilest, and obscurest Causes; And this is never more verified than in Courts, and the Issues of publick Affairs, whereof I could produce from my own Knowledge and Observation, three or four very Surprizing Instances' (*P.W.* viii. 172). Similarly in *The Conduct of the Allies* (1711) Swift attributes the whole course of the War of the Spanish Succession to the chance circumstance that the Duke of Marlborough happened to be a general rather than an admiral (*P.W.* vi. 23).

One of the examples that Swift uses in *Gulliver's Travels*, the death of Alexander the Great, had interested him since at least 1712. When raised by the magician, Alexander assures Gulliver 'upon his Honour that he was not poisoned, but dyed of a Fever by excessive Drinking' (III. vii. 195). In February 1712 Swift had written to Stella that 'I came home early, and have read 200 Pages of Arrian, Alexdr the great is just dead; I do not think he was poisoned. Betwixt you and me all those are but idle Storyes, tis certain that neither Ptolemy nor Aristobulus thought so, and they were both with him when they [slip for he] died. Tis a Pity we have not their Historyes' (*J.S.* ii. 501). The example of Alexander both exposed the unreliability of 'secret history' and gave a suitably mundane real cause of his death, excessive drinking.

The climax of Gulliver's stay with the magician is the calling up of 'some *English* Yeomen of the old Stamp . . . once so famous for the Simplicity of their Manners, Dyet and Dress' and other virtues (III. viii. 201). Gulliver and the reader are moved by 'how all these pure native Virtues were prostituted for a Piece of Money by their Grand-children; who in selling their Votes, and managing at Elections have acquired every

Vice and Corruption that can possibly be learned in a Court'
(III. viii. 201-2). When we compare the picture of these
corrupt descendants of the old yeomen with the satisfactory
'general Composition' that has been achieved in Brobdingnag,
we are naturally led to ponder how Swift can consistently
hold a theory of cycles of decay and renewal with a belief in
the possibility of the clock being somehow stopped, as apparently in Brobdingnag. Swift is nowhere very explicit about
this. The answer may be found in Swift's reading of Harrington. For in *Oceana* (with which Brobdingnag has so much in
common) Harrington seems to suppose that the achievement
of a permanent balance of property and, therefore, of political power would arrest the process of degeneration. In *Oceana*
the principles of limited landholdings and rotation in office
create a permanent pool of independent landholders to
provide a collective check on the encroaching tendencies of
the executive.[24] But *Gulliver's Travels* is a satire, not a
treatise, and its political theories should not be subjected to
quite the same scrutiny as is appropriate for a work like
Oceana.

Swift's critique of contemporary society is radical in scope
while deeply conservative in its basis. His ideal is an early
Renaissance state, freed from the slavery and superstition of
the Middle Ages and yet untroubled, if not untouched, by
the wider reaches of the disturbing discoveries which in a
short while transformed Europe. At the end of the *Travels*
Gulliver refers to the Brobdingnagians as 'the least corrupted'
of the Yahoo societies he has visited, and he commends their
'wise Maxims in Morality and Government' (IV. xii. 292).
They seem arrested at an early stage of the Renaissance: they
have printing but make little use of it, they have not discovered any new worlds with their attendant complications.
Thus Brobdingnag should be seen not so much as a practical
scheme for reform in contemporary England as a nostalgic
evocation of a vanished golden age. It is happily exempt, for
example, from the vexations of foreign policies. Nevertheless,
there are parts of the politics of Brobdingnag that it might
still 'be our Happiness to observe' (IV. xii. 292), and they

---

[24] *Oceana*, in *Political Works*, ed. Pocock, pp. 183-8.

are the politics of common sense. How far Swift's common-sense solutions might have worked in contemporary society we shall never know, for they were never tried. But they certainly helped ensure the success of *Gulliver's Travels* as imaginative literature. As a means of exposing nonsense and folly, common sense is excellent: it provides a widely accepted (if not always practised) norm that requires no special arguing for. And, in the end, it is for its satire, not its solutions, that we read *Gulliver's Travels*.

Index